Dawn Cogger, the mother of three adult children, grandmother, retired nurse and spiritual director, emigrated from Canada as a young girl to the United States. She worked in Paediatrics and Long-Term Care as well as other areas. Providing spiritual direction for individuals and retreats has been a labour of love for most of her adult life. Dawn never dreamed she would write, let alone be published. Her experiences of life realities inspired her to journal, fostering growth beyond her fears. Daily walks and painting with watercolours and acrylics keep her learning in joy. Her love of nature, including Canada's Lake Superior, and searching for God, continue in parallel. Dawn has been published in Presence, an International Journal of Spiritual Direction. She has been published in the anthology, Corners: Voices on Change. She lives in Wisconsin with her husband.

Dedicated to my children and their families, and to all who provide the gift of listening.

Dawn Cogger

WOMB TO TOMB TO WOMB

Holy Longing

AUSTIN MACAULEY PUBLISHERS™

LONDON • CAMBRIDGE • NEW YORK • SHARJAH

A CIP catalogue record for this title is available from the British Library.

ISBN 9781398454040 (Paperback)
ISBN 9781398454064 (ePub e-book)
ISBN 9781398454057 (Audiobook)

www.austinmacauley.com

First Published 2023
Austin Macauley Publishers Ltd®
1 Canada Square
Canary Wharf
London
E14 5AA

I am grateful to writers Sandy Benitez and Amy Cordova at Split Rock arts program, the University of Minnesota; to writer and editor, Amy Lou Jenkins at Write by the Lake, University of Wisconsin; writer Julie Tallard Johnson at Write by the Light, University of Wisconsin; Laurie Scheer, manuscript coach, Write by the Lake, University of Wisconsin; and Grace Wilson of College of the Albemarle, North Carolina. All these writers/teachers inspired, affirmed and honed my writing. I thank Editor Nick Wagner of Presence, an international journal of spiritual direction, and the editorial board, who read and asked me to rewrite my first reflection in 2010 in first person, my first publication, my first owning of my voice. I thank Helen Michaels, playful woman of wisdom. I thank my husband, Bill, who kept my computer working, encouraged new computer skills, and trusted my process of time and energy. Finally, I want to thank all the people who contributed towards the publication of this book with their wisdom and expertise, especially the staff at Austin Macauley Publishers.

Table of Contents

Holy Longing

Our St Barnabas Hospital School of Nursing class of 1964, regally processed into the Episcopal Cathedral Church of St Mark in Minneapolis, Minnesota. We walked together in white uniforms, white caps with black stripes, wearing corsages of deep red roses, exhibiting pride and joy.

A flash of memories of classes at Macalester College, our Capping ceremony at St Marks, nursing labs, sitting in our dorm rooms telling jokes to survive the impending exams, and sagas of boyfriends and family concerns jogged through my memory.

We sang, *Go heal the sick and suffering, it is the Lord's command.* (Author Unknown)

My long-time dream of becoming a nurse was now a reality.

O

Upon nursing graduation, we faced state boards for licensure as registered nurses. Because our paediatric instructor was disorganised and sounded unsure in lectures, I didn't feel confident in my paediatric knowledge. I re-read the book and experiential notes.

After taking state boards in Madison, Wisconsin, it took six weeks to get results. The results came by mail, USPS. With all my being, I hoped I passed. I opened the envelope fearing failure. I passed. Paediatrics was my highest score. My license was honoured in both Wisconsin and Minnesota. Indeed, I was happy. I planned to move back home to work in Wisconsin, then go back to Minnesota to work, and possibly more school at Macalester College.

I wanted a position in paediatrics. Because the local Wisconsin hospital didn't have paediatric openings, I accepted a position in the Newborn Nursery (no Neo-Natal Intensive Care Unit, NICUs then). I worked days and evening shifts. Most days, our newborn nursery had twenty babies. Because it was 1964, fathers weren't allowed in delivery rooms. Babies were always in the nursery unless it was feeding time.

It was fun to watch eager parents view their newborn babies through the windows. If one of us had time, we'd pick up the baby to give a better view or roll the bassinette closer to the window.

It was AWESOME…to be handed a newborn by the labour and delivery nurse, to bathe and examine the usually healthy baby as the baby announced its entry into the world. It was amazing to see how each baby was unique in all ways, including temperament.

It was rewarding to bring the newborn baby to the mother, to allow, to watch, to help her unwrap her baby, to watch her look and feel fingers, toes, hair, and to interact with her long-awaited gift.

We also had challenges of birth defects such as a cleft lip. Those first newborn days were observed for difficulties with breast or bottle feeding, sleeping, and responsiveness. We provided education. We facilitated the beginning of a new family.

○

A premature infant, weighing less than two pounds, died on the day shift before I arrived to work the evening shift. My head nurse said, "Her body needs to go to the morgue." She said this without a trace of tenderness. *Is that how you become after years of doing this work?* I thought.

"How do I do that?" I asked as my thoughts returned to the task, holding back fear.

"Go downstairs, you'll see the morgue. Put her in the small refrigerator." Finding my way through quiet white corridors, I was aware of the lifeless form wrapped in a soft pink blanket in my arm. I saw the sign, *MORGUE*. I was scared. I opened the heavy door to a spotlessly clean room with the shine of stainless-steel glaring. No bodies and no people in sight. I saw the small refrigerator. I didn't want to linger. I opened the blanket with hesitancy, not knowing what I'd feel. I saw a perfect-looking baby, small but perfect. I touched her petite hands, letting her miniature fingers slide over my index finger. I noticed her perfect face with eyes closed in peace. My heart started to rip. *Babies aren't supposed to die!* I wrench my thoughts back to my task, my job. I re-wrapped her securely, tucking the blanket around her. I wondered if I'm supposed to take the blanket off and bring it back to the nursery. I ignored the thought. I carefully placed her in the refrigerator. I wanted to keep holding her, to weep and wail, to yell out my anger while saying goodbye. I remember I want to do a good job, to do as I'm told, to be responsible. I remember I had twenty-five other babies, and parents to attend to that evening shift and how I was to conduct myself. I couldn't feel this now and perform eight hours of work. I composed myself and walked away.

After my shift was complete, I drove home with a mixture of gratitude of how I got through work, even a sense of pride and disbelief, of the first child death experience that ever happened.

◯

In 1961, while sitting in the lounge between classes with my nursing peers at Macalester College, I experienced an unexpected kiss on the side of my neck. The person had come from behind. I turned my head in surprised inquiry to see an unknown smiling young man, and a laughing former high school classmate...then clueless he would become my husband. We talked enough to know we were both students. Shortly thereafter, early in his freshman year, I heard he left Macalester College and joined the United States Army.

Years later, he came home to Wisconsin after his military tour in Vietnam. I finished my nursing education and had come back to Wisconsin too. I planned to work while I temporarily lived with my parents. He, my husband to be, was considering going back to Vietnam for another two years. He learned I was working in the area and called. We started dating, catching up on the years between any contacts.

We danced to live music in a Wisconsin tavern. He liked to dance. He liked to drink beer. I sipped enough to be able to stay and dance. We both loved rock 'n roll. We watched a movie at his mum's home with their Pekinese dog who barked any time we embraced. We ate dinner with his mother. His father had died when he was in high school. His mother and I talked while we did dishes and while he worked on his new stereo set. I was happy to be dating but knew I would soon be leaving. To his mother's dismay, he was still considering another military tour.

I moved back to Minnesota for my new welcomed job in paediatrics. Initially, I had a one-room apartment within walking distance of the hospital. I didn't have a car. Work was my focus. After several months, two high school peers and a co-worker from my job in Wisconsin were able to rent a house together. I bought a blue Ford Fairlane.

My future spouse decided to decline the additional military service and moved to Minnesota for school and work. We dated sporadically at first, then more. One evening an engagement ring was nestled within a bouquet of flowers. I was thrilled.

My fiancé and I married in the fall of 1967 in a church service with seventy family and friends in Wisconsin. I wore a lovely long, white gown my mum helped me buy in Minneapolis. My dad walked me down the aisle. My sister and my husband's brother-in-law stood up for us. We had a weekend honeymoon before we got back to work for me and work and school for him in Minneapolis. We rented a one-bedroom lower level of an older home in Minneapolis near a park, St Mary's Hospital, and the Mississippi River.

When we married, I decided to leave hospital work for work in long-term care. I thought it would give us a better start in our life together. I could work full-time days instead of revolving shifts, often double shifts of sixteen hours. My new position evolved into the education of staff, which I loved and meant I kept up on education for myself as well. I loved my job and found I loved geriatrics and the care. My nursing career grew, with classes held at Sister Kenny Institute in

Minneapolis, Minnesota, to include care of people with spinal cord injuries. From there, I changed jobs to full-time Head Nurse at the newly constructed Extended Care Center near our home. It was a challenge I wanted. In a brand-new building, I started as Head Nurse in the Extended-Care Unit, which involved seventy patients on three adjoining wings. One wing became the beginnings of an Alzheimer's unit, one wing had patients that needed extended care while they received physical, occupational and speech therapies. Many of those patients had a stroke (more prevalent then), a fracture or a heart attack. One wing had patients receiving treatment for cancer (oncology), the trial for then the experimental drug, L-Dopa for Parkinson's disease, and spinal cord injuries.

In less than two years after our marriage, my husband quit his electrical engineering program at the University before completion. He worked at the University, too. I was devastated. I felt betrayed as we'd agreed I'd work full-time and he'd go to school, working part-time at the University. Because I knew my parents would be upset about him not getting his degree, my innards were in silent turmoil. He re-started school at an electrical technical college, but he wanted to explore other avenues such as working as a cook in a high-end restaurant. He had a dream of owning his own restaurant. The restaurant work involved many hours starting as an assistant, preparing food in the morning, then cooking meals late in the evening. That particular restaurant work ended after several months of arduous hours in the kitchen heat. He lost weight. He went on to his next work.

For fun, we camped in northern Wisconsin. We loved the night's dark quiet beside a rippling stream. We loved the early morning sun with our dog in the tent with us. We learned to fly-fish. Our dog quietly watched, then barked as our excitement rose when the fly-rod bent. My husband's waders almost filled as he tried to get the net under my catch.

Life became fuller. We moved to a three-bedroom home. In the following years, we had three children. I worked part-time, continuing at the Extended Care Center after the children were born. My husband had full-time work.

After three-plus years of marriage, early morning labour took us to the hospital. I was given a deep injection while in labour due to a high blood pressure reading that hadn't previously shown up. My husband rubbed my back during my contractions. The doctor checked me. He thought it would be a while before delivery. He left for lunch. My husband left for lunch, too. Twenty minutes later, I was in delivery. Our son was small and somewhat premature. At the doctor's request, the nurse whisked my son away, without me having a glance. With no warning, anaesthesia put me out.

We weren't sure how premature our son was because I had bled mid-pregnancy. There were no ultrasounds then. Though our son was able to breathe on his own and nurse from a preemie nipple, he was kept in an incubator in the nursery for a month.

On delivery day, because of my high blood pressure, I wasn't allowed to go to the nursery, even by wheelchair, though I felt good. I was discharged on the morning of day three. My empty arms and heart ached as I left the hospital room to our home's empty crib. While a patient, I'd been allowed in the hospital nursery ONCE to put my hands on my newborn son. He was a perfect baby. I wanted to stay with him forever. He weighed about three pounds. He couldn't come home until he was five pounds-eight ounces. (Today, my husband and I would have been able to hold him, feed him, and he would have come home at three pounds) I wanted to nurse him. I hand pumped my breasts and brought my beginning milk to the nursery. I think they threw it out. I was considered contaminated as soon as I was discharged home. It was incredibly painful. I cried and cried feeling a part of me had been cut off and would never be given back. I called the nursery every day to see how our son was and what he weighed. My emotions vacillated with his weight. I was a nurse. I had worked with new-borns. I wanted to smash the door and take him. I had to force feelings away to function.

My husband didn't share or show his feelings about our gain or loss. He had refused to go to childbirth classes with me. It was the beginning of fathers being allowed in the delivery room. No tears came from him. I was numb. My parents called to find out their grandson's weight. My mother-in-law had a soft tone of concern when she called because I hadn't written or called except when he was firstborn.

Friends from work wanted to have the baby shower they had planned to happen three weeks before his birth. As they arrived three weeks after his birth, I received welcoming hugs. We received gifts. It was held in our home. Silent tears ran with good-bye hugs. Breast milk stained my light green dress.

When our son came home after a whole month, my husband picked him up...this was my husband's first time being with his son. He walked in delight with his son cupped in his hands and showed him his new home. Our baby moved his eyes to look at everything.

I tried to nurse him. He turned his head and fussed; my breast was foreign to him. My husband said, "He doesn't want it." I had to let it go.

Soon thereafter, our son was baptised in a private ceremony at St Paul's Episcopal Church in Minneapolis. Since we didn't have a church home at the time, I asked an Episcopal priest I worked with at the Catholic Extended Care Center. The priest told me he wanted us to be a part of a church community, for us and for our son. He said he would, however, do the baptism. A friend of both my husband and I who we knew from high school, and her husband, were my son's sponsors, called Godparents. Godparents, along with parents, promise to support faith development in the life of the child. I never said but feared hell for my son if he wasn't baptised. My husband had no concern either way and willingly went along.

To be home with our baby, I left my head nurse position and started working part-time nights. I slept a little in between. I laid on the couch with our son in a playpen beside me to take a nap. In the evening hours, I tried to rest before work. I awakened whenever he made a sound even though his dad cared for him. We needed more income in addition to my husband's full-time income. I also wanted to keep up with my profession. New medications and treatments were constantly evolving.

Two and a half years later, we had a girl. (Still no ultrasound tests). My mum came before the birth so she could be with our son while I was in the hospital. I was grateful. Mum and I had a special day away from the house, with my husband home with our son. We browsed the Minneapolis downtown stores including Dayton's. Mum loved to look at their furniture. I enjoyed the walk and sights on the gorgeous May Day knowing we'd soon have a new baby. With my first-born son and my second pregnancy, pregnant women were to keep total weight gain to twenty pounds. It was hard. How I hated to get on the scale at each prenatal visit, and I was hungry. While shopping, my mum realised my energy was waning. She insisted, and we had ice cream cones. It was great.

Again, my husband was with me in labour, not delivery. I had a compassionate doctor who was aware of the circumstances of my first pregnancy. I was afraid I'd deliver prematurely again. He reassured me premature labour was not likely to be repeated. Instead, since I'd been dilated for weeks, I was induced.

The process worked into delivery. My doctor immediately placed our healthy newborn daughter on my abdomen before dealing with the afterbirth. Tears of joy ran as I quietly thanked God for a healthy daughter. I loudly thanked my dear doctor for the incredible gift of my warming, wriggling baby on my belly. That warm energy penetrated my soul.

My mum visited me at the hospital. She came angry. She told me my son DID take a nap, while my husband said he didn't nap. There were no words of joy nor questions about me. I was glad when she left. I felt pulled between her and my husband.

I continued to work evenings or nights part-time. When my husband cared for our children, he called it, *babysitting*. He didn't consider it partner parenting, not an unusual view at that time.

We belonged to the Presbyterian Church near our home. I was involved in church school. Our month-old daughter was baptised during our church service, supported by other congregants. We sang, *Morning Has Broken.* (E. Farjeon)

Seven years after our daughter was born, a young neighbour friend of my son's said I looked like I carried a large watermelon while I willingly mowed the lawn in the hot August sun. I was beyond the due date and hoping to soon deliver. The melon turned out to be another full-term healthy girl. Again, I wanted my husband to attend childbirth classes. I so wanted him to be with me in delivery. He refused. No discussion. I hoped it would bring us closer together, too. No ultrasounds yet so we didn't know the sex until birth. We had the delight of surprise; we were grateful for our healthy baby girl.

My husband's nebulous, indifferent views hadn't shifted about God and church. We had moved to a suburb of Minneapolis. I changed jobs. I decided to change churches too. I was now an active member at St Mark's Episcopal Church. At age three, our youngest daughter was baptised as I held her. My husband and friends were there. Our friends were dear neighbours, delighted to be her sponsors.

While my youngest daughter was an infant, I was offered a full-time position in a long-term care facility where I already worked part-time. The position was Director of Staff Development and Infection Control. Thankfully, after weeks of investigating childcare, a relative of another employee became my daughter's almost grandmotherly caregiver. I wanted the teaching position.

○

An ad announcing a class for nursing staff caught my attention. The class offering was about grief and loss regarding the loss of a child. I decided to attend. As Director of Staff Development, I planned to bring the information back to our staff and allow them to share personal and professional experiences.

A man whose 16-year-old son had died started the class. He described his journey. His journey of death, the shock of how others reacted sometimes adding to the pain, and how he started to heal. He talked about initially feeling he was in a fog, a few feet off the ground, observing what was going on in life but not participating in it. He said he finally went to counselling and spent most of the time crying in a safe place. Since then, he and his wife, who was present, formed a support group for people who had lost a child.

While the father talked, I remembered a young boy who died in my care a few years after graduation, when I worked in a children's hospital in Minnesota.

As the father spoke, I started to cry. I couldn't stop. I stayed as long as I could tolerate myself in disarray. I left class and went home.

I was in my late thirties, married with three children. Once home, I decided to catch up on laundry and hang the clothes outside for the fresh air and sunshine. While hanging the clothes in the brightness and breeze of the glorious day, tears dripped. Memories came one after the other. The memories came from the depths of silence. Memories turned into a vision.

The children's hospital had a medical unit, a surgical unit and an isolation unit. I worked mainly on the medical unit as a medication and treatment nurse on the day shift unless the Head Nurse was off, in which case, I assumed the Head Nurse role. When I worked the evening shift or night shift, I was the nurse in charge.

"They can't figure out what's wrong," I was told in a report as Evening Charge Nurse. "He's in isolation. We're doing tests. His chest keeps filling up with fluid." For days we watched our teenage patient, our boy. I listened to his day nurse as she described how quietly brave and accepting her patient was with tests that were painful and sometimes humiliating. She told me how frustrated she was and how she was hurting. All of us had a sense of rising concern bordering on feelings of powerlessness. This was decades before we have CT scans and Ultrasounds. X-rays showed little. The physician was puzzled because there were no clear signs to lead to an answer. He was trying to avoid unnecessary surgery.

After days of no change, surgery was scheduled. No one mentioned the word God, but everyone prayed for our boy in their own way.

After eight hours in the surgical suite, the physician walked from the grey double doors to the nursing station. All our inquisitive, concerned eyes focused on him. The physician's lack of smile and distant looking eyes spoke of emptiness and fatigue. With tears choking his voice, he said he needed someone to special our boy (to take care of only him). Our boy's primary day nurse, who was getting ready to leave, softly said she couldn't stay. With a greater softness, said, "I couldn't stay anyway."

I had worked the day shift. I briefly and quietly considered caring for our boy for the additional eight hours. There weren't any extra staff for the evening shift. I decided I'd stay, not really sure why.

Minutes later, surgical staff wheeled our boy out of surgery to his private room leaving him on the gurney to avoid more trauma of transferring him to his bed. Two medical students accompanied him.

The two students worked diligently, even frantically. Medication after medication was injected into his IV (intravenous site) and his pale skin. I couldn't keep up with recording the names and doses on paper as they asked for them. I provided them with the bottles and syringes. Our sandy-haired boy laid motionless. I wondered what they found. There was no time to talk, only to provide for those tending to him.

"We can't do anymore," one student said to the other in a tone of defeat. They stopped. They left the room.

The room was silent. No breathing was heard except my own. I stood looking at the boy in disbelief, wanting to cry out, scream, *My God, no, why? Damn, dammit. God, God, please God, no please God, no!*

I wilted with exhaustion, an empty shell. I looked at his perfect face. I straightened his white sheet. I started cleaning up the mess of syringes, medications and other looks of dishevelment. In doing so, I didn't have to think about the emptiness in his body and mine. There was no concept of time, only a silent screaming moment.

Our boy's parents entered the space; glanced at me and in unison, moved to our boy. His mother leaned over him. She embraced his face in her hands. I said, very quietly, "I'm sorry." Almost hoping they wouldn't hear. I wasn't sure how they'd respond. I had no idea what to do. I stood aside. I wished I could disappear into the green walls and allow them to be alone.

His mother said, "He was the best..." and cried in quiet anguish. She held his face and kissed him on his still fair cheeks.

His father touched him, speechless. His other arm was around his wife. I sensed a searing pain that can never be given words. Disbelief pervaded the room.

My insides struggled...in my gut, mind and heart. The inner movements were all over the place wanting to be able to do something to fix this terrible nightmare. *I'm a nurse! I'm supposed to be able to support people, to protect, to make a difference. And how do I do THAT God? How do I do THAT? Do something!*

I tuck away the turmoil. The boy's parents left.

O

The loss of our boy, the loss of the infant girl, and the loss of dreams ran with my tears.

I stood in bright daylight between the front window and our double bed. I was in my nightgown, wine-coloured velour robe and slippers.

My mind was debating. I felt I was unknown to myself. I felt gaping holes in my bleeding heart; absurd. Tears came. I cried for days. A myriad of feelings after years of unacknowledged grief flowed like a rushing dangerous waterfall. It seemed a dam, now broken, had protected my heart. (Cogger) The gaping fracture got wider and wider. From the opening came every drop of water, every creek, every river of tarnished and painful life. Anger appeared too. It rushed in a torrent as though it never had an outlet. It was frightening. *I can't do any more than I have. There is no way I can do it anymore. How can I give myself to God? I can't imagine doing it anymore. Yet, hell, I do fear hell. How can hell be any worse? I've tried to be the perfect mother, wife, nurse and daughter. I keep failing. I'm impatient and screaming at my children just like my mum did! I hate myself. I feel that if I died at this moment, everyone would walk over me; my husband, my children...they wouldn't notice. Suicide...I know it's wrong hell is the result. I don't want my kids (12, 10 and 3 years old) to suffer the loss; the betrayal. Do I kill them to protect them from the pain of their mother committing suicide and being left without her? I AM CRAZY. I'm worthless and disposable. God, God please help me. I can't do it anymore. I can't do it anymore. Hell? Is it real? I can't begin to imagine being more submissive to God, works and others.*

With a twist of anger, I said, "I won't give YOU (my mum) the satisfaction of suicide."

In terror and despair, I decide to leap; to give myself to God. God, the relentless overseer expecting perfection, performance, efficiency, pleasing everyone, perfection, perfection, perfection. I'm instantly ready to leap into the abyss, certain I will die.

Instead of meeting God, the relentless, harsh judge. Behind my left shoulder, I hear, "I'm here," spoken in a soft comforting sincere tone. It came in an essence of gentility I've never known that is penetrating. *It's Jesus. I've never communicated with Jesus. I've had God in my life but not Jesus. I've heard his name, heard stories in Sunday school and church but I haven't associated with him.*

I fell to my knees by our bed. In my heart, mind and soul I gave all to God…all of me. I, who have failed in all realms as the mother I wanted to be. Nothing has turned out right – marriage, work, or me.

All my values were erased. All I'd been taught and believed, all my hopes and dreams, all of everything. I gave it all to God. I thought I was going to die – by the hand of God – by guillotine…death by God.

After I said, "I give me to YOU, all of my life." I had a sense of standing naked on a high mountain. I'd been plucked from a sinkhole of muck – quicksand covered me, and I was going under. I was brought to a strong pinnacle where the muck of my life was washed away with gentle rain. I was naked, cold, shivering, frightened and now, warmed by the sun. God knew everything about me. He could see everything. I was transparent. I was amazed I was alive; that I had been cleansed of the muck. I wasn't struck down. I was being warmed and alive.

○

From that moment on, I started walking baby steps of a deeper faith with a merciful God new to me. I felt infinite gratitude for being forgiven, for being alive, for a sense of gentle acceptance, though I felt God's desires and my dreams didn't match; it was totally God's way. I knew Jesus was with me, both awesome and frightening. I had a quiet, powerful sense of God and a sense that God was ALL. I wanted to know more.

I didn't share my experience with my husband, children, parents, siblings, or anyone. I felt it would just confirm their sense I was crazy. I felt an unspoken need to protect myself in my infancy of a deeper faith. I felt any talk would simply bring more rejection from my family of origin, immediate family, and others. Yet, I felt a new strength, courage, and knowing in my bones.

○

My hunger for God was insatiable. I read about God. I talked with God. I felt the humility of God's mercy, again and again, bringing tears. I related to Mary Magdalene; her demons (afflictions), her humility, and her great love for Christ. I didn't feel alone. My behaviour started to change.

I was able to be more patient with myself and my children, no longer yelling and admonishing them as I had expected instant performance and perfection. I was able to forgive myself for not being able to do all I thought I should. I now realised sometimes I had no control over life. Sometimes life led to another person's disappointment in me, which I previously found devastating. I now had more understanding for others who let me down.

I put judging, in any way, on the shelf, feeling my entire life was up to God. I thought God was a presence outside myself with an agenda for me I didn't know or needed to understand. I noticed behaviour and words from others. When other people said something about God or prayer, I listened, heard, and took what was fit for me.

I wanted to share my experience with others because it dramatically changed my life. I knew it wouldn't be accepted at home; just as scripture indicates in the RSV Bible, Luke 4:24, that you're not honoured as a prophet in your own land.

I wanted to give to others what I'd been given, yet not become a zealot. A zealot was a person who turned other people off, as it had for me when God or Jesus was pushed at me, especially when I was struggling. It was a platitude made without any listening; pushed in my face as though it solved all problems.

○

As I said previously, because we moved in 1976 to a northern suburb of Minneapolis when my son was five, and my daughter two, I decided to leave the Presbyterian Church we had attended before my last child was born. I became a parishioner at St Mark's Cathedral Episcopal Church. At first, I resisted my own thoughts and desires in regard to the church, thinking it would be my mum's choice. I loved the sacramental church with the powerful organ music and the liturgy. It was where I was capped and graduated as a nurse. I decided it's what I wanted.

I realised the chains put around me by my parents, and myself were now breaking.

In a phone call from the church coordinator of children's education, who asked if I'd volunteer to teach, I learned she too was spiritually hungry. Her house sounded alive, vibrating actually, with the wrestling of three boys and their friends, as she chuckled.

We met weekly at a fast-food restaurant with a cup of tea. We shared what we read and learned about ourselves from the book, *Our Many Selves*, by Elizabeth O'Conner.[1] Our friendship was a gift of sharing all realms of life. Our hopes, dreams, grief, and questioning were held in sacred honesty and trust.

Since my profound experience with Jesus in 1983, I had considered ordination as an Episcopal priest. (Women's ordination in the Episcopal Church began in 1974) I read the requirements for seminary, for a Divinity Degree. I read and observed the expectations of the lives of our parish priests. At the same time, I was working as a nurse.

I had a telling experience with a patient. I was assisting my patient to clean up and put on regular daily clothes because his minister was coming to visit him at his hospital bedside. Prior to dressing, the patient shared his fears and pain with me while we tended to basic needs. He sat on the toilet, needing a nurse's supervision and support for his surgically altered body. Some of his words were about God. He wondered if he was being punished. I doubt he shared the concerns with his minister. Instead, he was getting ready to look all-together.

I couldn't imagine the amount of further study needed for ordination with my family of husband and three children. I couldn't imagine the amount of being on call as a priest, every day. I decided motherhood and nursing were where I belonged, however, I still had a hunger to share in a new way.

I attended an all-day conference on spiritual care for nurses. It was well timed. I bought the book, *Spiritual Care: The Nurse's Role* by Sharon Fish and Judith Allen (Fish). Assessment of a patient to assist with the patient's whole life and health included examining the physical body and listening to answers about the person's present and past life. That included noting the pictures in the patient room, cards, food choices, interests, language, religion and culture. It's looking at the totality of life.

The spirituality class for nurses affirmed my sense that '*God loves us in spite of ourselves, not because of who we are or what we do.*' (Fish) God truly was more understanding, more merciful than anyone I ever met; more understanding than I ever imagined.

○

About that same time in 1983, I read an article in the Minneapolis Star Tribune Newspaper about spiritual direction. I'd never heard of it. *That's what I want to do.* It told about the ministry of listening to others to facilitate their faith in God.

A few months later, there was an invitation from the Women's Group in the St Mark's Newsletter of the Episcopal Cathedral Church of St Mark in Minneapolis. St Mark's was now my parish. The invitation was to hear parishioner, Ollie Rose Olsen (now deceased), speak about spiritual direction. It was a noonday meeting. Somehow, with three children and full-time work, I got there. I listened with full attention. I heard about listening, with God's love to another person; and thereby, God working to lead to a deeper faith.

The spiritual director spoke in soft tones of strength. She spoke with a supportive gentleness. Her essence and words brought a desire to talk with her further. I approached her and told her I'd like to learn more about spiritual direction. She asked me to call her and come to her home to talk with her. She said, "I noticed your head lifted up when we prayed in the group."

I called her. She welcomed me into her home. She asked me what brought me to her. The question led me to describe my experiences. I told her of my desire for God when I was a little girl and how it was not talked about in my family. In fact, it was ridiculed by others. I told her about my experience of surrendering to God in despair and fear. I told her Jesus came behind my left shoulder and spoke to me. I said I'd been forgiven for everything in my life when I expected to die by God's hand or my own. I'd considered suicide, even homicide. I told her how I'd gone to a family 12-step group to be a good wife. When I saw the 12-steps, I said, "I've done that...that's what I've done." By that, I meant the surrender to a higher power and following the 12-steps.

She listened intently for many minutes not interrupting. When I told her, "Spiritual direction is what I want to do."

She said, "You must take care of yourself first."

She briefly told me about the Cenacle Retreat House in Wayzata, Minnesota, run by the Sisters of the Cenacle. She said I could call and ask for an application. She kept it simple. I was grateful.

I called the Cenacle Retreat House and filled out the application. It asked: my name, age, marital status, number of children, when was I able to meet and the name of my church community. It said to simply describe in a timeline and words, when I felt close to or far away from God, and how did I pray. It asked whether I wanted a person who was part of the religious community or a layperson as my director. I asked for the layperson, Ollie Rose who I heard and spoke to.

○

My Spiritual Director and I met every two weeks for six weeks to see how we fit together. Were we both comfortable? We both agreed to keep meeting.

When we first met, she asked me to share with her from my latest journal. She said, "You've lived in the spiritual world a lot." She asked me to bring any topic or concern to spiritual direction. We both were aware of God in our midst; God was the true director. She listened and listened and listened. She asked me how I saw God. She asked me how I was praying. She affirmed life-giving behaviour. I always felt heard. I wasn't afraid. I began to see my own truth by sharing and listening to myself. She modelled God's love and patience.

○

During this time of change, and my new seeking, I wasn't sure how or what to tell my husband about the Cenacle and spiritual direction. I told him what I was doing in the most factual way I could. I said I wanted to take more classes. I used the word spiritual. His response was no response, no questions, no affirmations and, no indication of saying no.

We'd been married sixteen years. We didn't discuss God. Years before he'd said he thought God was a crutch for people – a weakness. He didn't support my efforts to take our children to church, though he agreed to their baptisms and was there. I knew by this time he didn't want to be involved in church.

When we married, I knew OF God, but I didn't KNOW God. I didn't know how vital church was to me because I didn't know who I was. (You'll hear more about the unknowing of myself.) Because my husband's family had been active in the Presbyterian Church, I took it for granted it would be important to him and how we would function.

When I looked back, I realised I was attracted to my husband because he had a beautiful smile. Because he had a zeal for life. Because he gave me attention. When he was interested in something, it got his full attention, until it didn't. He liked to dance. He worked on projects such as woodworking. He didn't care what my mum thought, a novel and intriguing idea to me. His mother was kind and interested in me.

I thought it was important to be open and tolerant of everyone. Basically, to me, it meant I had no opinions, didn't know my desires, and certainly wouldn't put them out there first. I thought spouses met each other's needs and worked side by side. I thought we'd be happy. My belief was our marriage would be different from what I had lived as a child. I wanted a happy marriage and loving relationships with my children more than anything else. Pleasing my husband meant to cook his meals, keep the house in order, change the beds and towels every week, wash, and put away clothes. I was to meet him when he came home from work dressed in fresh clothes, with a smile and make him feel desired. I was to be available in all ways. I thought we would have children. Children would fit into our life as well as me working as a nurse if I wished. I thought he would support me in those dreams.

O

During my quiet time after my initial purification by God, I climbed into God's lap as a young child who cried and cried, not really knowing why, but felt held in safety and compassion. Sometimes I was the woman I was, in God's embrace that didn't let go until I was ready, or God and I sat facing each other with our hands clasped in mutual trust. God was always "there" for me. Later, I learned that God was "here" for me too – within or right beside me.

My needs in a relationship, in marriage, were more than any person could fill. What I was beginning to learn in God's 24 hours/7 days a week of compassion, love and attention, was that my life had some meaning. I sought counselling.

○

It was frightening, and against my whole upbringing to call and make my appointment for counselling. Growing up rules, spoken and unspoken, were to behave, dress properly, have impeccable manners, do as I was told, we don't have problems in our family, we don't ask for help, we certainly don't tell other people what is going on.

At first, I started with one-to-one therapy. The therapist told me about the book, *the Drama of the Gifted Child,* by Alice Miller. The book described how as a young child, even as an infant, the infant can sense the needs of the mother, (or caregiver). When the mother isn't able to reflect the interest and care for the infant the infant behaves accordingly to fulfil the parent's needs. The book helped me understand the woundedness of my parents, especially my mum. Understanding and healing of my own wounds came much later.

I was referred to adult group therapy for abused and neglected children. The six weekly sessions provided a subject such as communication. With presentations by counsellors, hand-outs, and group sharing, unhealthy and healthy boundaries and ways of interacting became clearer.

My current struggles of not ever feeling loved by my parents, my concerns in my marriage, and my concerns about my children came into the light even more.

I learned not to expect the abuser to own any part of my pain. However, I decided to write separate letters to my parents. I confronted my dad about how I felt abandoned by him when he started to travel, and that I had to deal alone with my mum. I told my mum her words were harsh, and I didn't feel loved, that I could never meet her expectations. I knew I may never hear from either parent again.

My dad wrote back in two weeks. He simply said, "I'm sorry I wasn't there for you." I cried with relief. My mum responded three months later. Her words were angry and defensive saying I didn't understand her and her life. There was no sensitivity for my feelings. Our counsellor had cautioned us about this, calling the response, *the velvet needle.* It meant, that the response given is supposedly with the softness of love, of velvet, but in reality, it's the abusive needle sting, again. It hurt, however, I really didn't expect it to be any different. I was learning and affirmed, that I lived in a dysfunctional family of origin. It was reality. I was learning to not let my mum be so important in my life, a grief in itself.

○

I shared what I learned in counselling with my Spiritual Director, Ollie Rose. She listened. She affirmed me for the courage to go to counselling. We again discussed whether we were a good fit for each other for spiritual direction. She suggested I pray aloud putting my own name in place of the prophet Isaiah, with the Bible's scripture from Isaiah 43 (America). The first five verses tell how God loves us, and how we are precious to God.

She asked, "Is there anything special you want to bring up?"

"Yes," I said as I started to cry thinking of the young patients I cared for. This time it was without the shame, or arrogance, of thinking I should have been able to do something to fix the situation of the death of a child.

"Can you ask Jesus to be with you?" she said. I was quiet. With my eyes closed, I silently extended Jesus an invitation while I allowed the morgue scene to be recreated in my mind.

I'm with the baby in the morgue. I sense a feeling of compassion for both the baby and me from Jesus. Jesus reaches out and takes her with a gentle smile. He wraps her in a warm blanket and takes her with him. *Thank you for her little life,* I think quietly, and I am comforted.

I envision cradling our boy's head in my left forearm, touching him with my left cheek and crying, raising my right hand to his head. I want God to give him a hug for me and tell him I love him. Tell him I'm glad he's been a part of my life. Again, I am comforted.

On another occasion, I shared the pain of my son's birth and his surgery when four months old. Ollie Rose asked if I could invite Mary, mother of Christ, to be with me. As I allowed the memory of my infant son, a scene came with him in surgery. My baby was on the surgical table with glaring lights. He was in the hands of a physician I hardly knew. I asked Mary to come, thinking she'd be with me. She did come. She appeared with my son, right by him. She touched him. She stayed with him. No one there was aware of her presence. My anxiety lifted. I trusted her. My son wasn't alone.

God's grace held my spiritual director and me as we met monthly for over fifteen years. Initially, I shared from journals I'd written to God. Years before, I'd read about journaling in the newspaper. The article said journaling – writing whatever came to mind – aided emotional healing and I wanted healing. I had also read and followed Julia Cameron's sage advice in, *the Artist's Way* (Cameron)to start each day with morning pages.

I told Ollie Rose about the letters I'd written my parents and their responses. I cried when I told her my dad said, "I'm sorry I wasn't there for you."

She said, "What's in those tears?" They were tears of relief, forgiveness and gratitude, which in that session, turned into love and respect for my dad. My dad had given me, without words, a love of nature which fed my spirit. To this day, I feel closest to God in nature. Dad and I never spoke about it. He accepted the hugs I initiated. He never spoke of God. I accepted Dad as he was.

○

My first retreat, soon after I started meeting with Ollie Rose, was at the Cenacle in Wayzata, Minnesota. The Cenacle was operated by the sisters of the Cenacle, the Roman Catholic women's religious community of the Society of Jesus (Jesuits). The sisters provide spiritual direction and retreats. Any seeker is welcome because Jesus invited EVERYONE to the Table.

The weekend retreat was about healing and our stages of spiritual growth. The leader was a Jesuit Priest, SJ (A priest in the Society of Jesus, a Roman Catholic religious community). I had spent time at the Cenacle in the chapel and library as well as with Ollie Rose. The retreat was a full weekend. Making this weekend a priority with my husband (who didn't understand a time away with God), children, and money-wise, was a significant step of courage for me to take care of me; do what I longed to do.

After being greeted, I was led to my room with a single bed, desk and a bathroom nearby. It was a safe, welcoming, clean quiet environment.

The retreat group met briefly with our facilitators on Friday evening after a simple silent meal with soft music playing. We were given suggested prayers. Saturday involved learning about families and spiritual growth. A healing service was offered after supper. I went. The Priest invited anyone who wanted healing to come forward. I came forward. Holding onto my tears, I said, "I want to ask God for forgiveness for considering suicide." As I stood, the Priest placed both his hands on my head. He prayed a simple prayer. As he prayed, I felt heat and pressure from his hands that permeated my being, releasing me from my past. I sat down, next to others. He asked us to anoint each other with provided oil. We did. We returned to the quiet of our rooms. I cried in relief, knowing God understood. I was forgiven and at peace. I slept. The next morning, we could talk at breakfast, getting to know those we'd prayed with and anointed. We ended with a service of thanksgiving.

The Director of the Cenacle, asked us to strip our beds before we left the retreat, putting the used linens in the pillowcase. (This is decades before COVID-19). While we remade the bed with fresh linens, she asked us to pray for the next (unnamed) person who would sleep in the bed. I often pray for a person as I make their bed, even my own.

○

In the early meetings with my spiritual director, my life was changing with my husband. Both my husband and I were faithfully attending 12-step programs. A few times, I went with him to a meeting at his request. It was toward a healthier life; however, the changes were painful. It felt like it was ripping us apart. Early in the 12-step program, I answered the questions about the personal inventory. The inventory described and indicated the personal depth of character traits. To my relief and joy, I learned I did have good character traits; I hadn't done EVERYTHING wrong. The 12-step program taught me to care for myself, and that self-care is not selfish. The program turned out to be one of the gifts my husband/our marriage gave me.

Through spiritual direction, I learned that going overboard with our good traits leads us to hurt others and ourselves. I learned everyone has a unique journey. I learned I had many idols. First, trying to be the daughter who was expected to be a person who knew how to do everything perfectly the first time. To be the nurse striving to keep every patient, every family member, healthy and happy. I tried to be the perfect loving mate, the perfect, loving parent, keep up our home, and volunteer at church and at school. My lifelong desires to be a nurse, have a happy marriage and have healthy

relationships with my children were my most ardent desires –
they were my heaven quest. Now I saw how our heaven
becomes our hell when we don't have God first.

After meeting monthly with my spiritual director for a
year, she told me about the Ignatian Exercises written by St
Ignatius of Loyola over 400 years ago.

○

I attended an evening program about the Spiritual Exercises of St Ignatius of Loyola (John English). Each person who had participated in the spiritual exercises shared their commitment to God and themselves; to pray for forty-five minutes each day and meet with their spiritual director every two weeks. They shared personal experiences of how praying with the scriptures about Jesus' life, using all their senses, within their ordinary life, facilitated seeing God in ordinary moments. It began the parallel journey of walking with Jesus, through our deaths (dying of ourselves) and resurrections (new beginnings).

I decided to participate in the school-year commitment.

During the Spiritual Exercises, I imagined the birth of Jesus. My prayer time, aware with all my senses, gave me a vision of the arduous journey, the fear and emptiness of no available rooms, the final place of birth in a stable, of how alone Mary and Joseph were. Did someone help, like another woman? Did Joseph help Mary though it was culturally taboo? My vision did show Joseph helped Mary. Finally, my imagination showed Mary held and adored her child, God's Son. When relating, as suggested by Ollie Rose, to ME being in Mary's arms myself, as her new-born child; God's love of us, we ordinary human beings, as daughters and sons, embraced me. I was adored and loved by Mary too; by God.

During the Episcopal liturgical time of Lent my Ignatian Exercise, quiet took me to the desert (Mark.1:12; Mt.4.1–1; Lk.4.1–13), (America) I saw Jesus had total trust in God; was tempted, and his relationship with God gave him everything he needed. Jesus resisted the temptations of power, wealth, and food. At the end of forty days in the desert, Jesus was weak. Angels ministered to him, displaying his humanity.

I heard a person involved in spiritual direction say women's temptations could be different than Jesus'. My temptations (sins) were: people-pleasing, self-pity, wanting to be perfect and hiding myself – my voice.

I felt I'd been in the desert for years with little support from my parents and marriage. There were no relatives, no grandparents to bring life to the desert either. Now I began to know the personal love of God and the gift of Christ. I saw God as Christ's parent. I felt the pain of my Saviour's (Christ's) suffering for me. I saw his mother, Mary, and friend, Mary Magdalene, and other women who were faithful, brave, and suffered on the journey with Christ, (John 19.25– 26) (America)as well as appreciated by Jesus.

After Jesus died and was taken from the cross, my meditation time brought Jesus' head cradled in my left arm. His body lay in the silence of death and peace. I knew death. I had held, touched, washed, cried and carried the dead, and I loved Jesus. Before Jesus died, I had the sense of God's unimaginable pain of watching his son die. To me, the darkness, the storm, was God crying out of the exquisite pain of Jesus' sacrifice, and hope, with God's and Jesus' commitments to humanity, to show us, The Relationship.

The Examen is an important part of the Spiritual Exercises of St Ignatius. The Examen is done daily. It awakens us to what gives us life (what adds to the fullness of your life?) and what takes away from your life (what took my energy away?). The Examen is done with an awareness of God's love and understanding. It is NOT about the judgement of a good or bad label or grade for ourselves. I usually do the Examen in the morning regarding the day before because that's when I'm most alert. I journal too. It's great if you can do the Examen at the end of your day, aware of what transpired in your day. One can ask, what was my high today or what gave me life today? The next question is what was my low today or what took away from my life today? The Exercise indicated what fed my life and what didn't. Out of gratitude for whatever came while sitting in God's compassion, led to healing. From there, I made choices for my life. How do I care for myself? How do I want to spend my time, money and energy? (Linn, Linn, Linn)

The Spiritual Exercises of St Ignatius helped me see God in everything. God's love and faithfulness entered my every pore. I now walked with Jesus, in his life, as he walked with me.

I viewed God as my Father, as father of all of us everywhere. God, my Father wants the best for everyone. That thought alone helped me to realise, and know God was available to everyone; a freeing thought for my sense of responsibility for everyone. Jesus, Jesus was not only my counsellor and redeemer but my brother, my friend.

○

After the school year of participating in the Ignatian Exercises, I applied to attend the three-year education program to become a Certified Spiritual Director through the Cenacle. I was ignorant about the cost. When I learned, what was a meagre cost for the education, but a challenge for me, I called the Cenacle Director. She was known as a forthright, firm-speaking Director of the Cenacle. I had high regard for her and at the same time, was afraid of her. She said to me, in an unexpected endearing tone sending love through the phone, "You can pay whatever you can, each payment. Just make sure it's more than fifty cents, which is what it costs us to record it."

While kneeling in ardent prayer in church at St Mark's, one of my dear friends, (a camping sister), whispered in my ear. "It will be paid for." She startled me. We quietly laughed.

○

The first year of the Cenacle three-year spiritual direction certification program was learning what spiritual direction is and isn't (it's not counselling).[2] As we were told in classes, spiritual direction is an ongoing, one-to-one relationship for a person who is hungry for prayer, wants to find God in their life, or have a deeper relationship with God. The person who comes to the spiritual direction (called directee or companion) brings (talks about) anything in their life. The director (companion or guide) listens with every fibre of being, noticing what brings life (or energy or movements toward or away from God). Both director and directee are aware of God's presence. Through the holy listening, the directee discovers how our ordinary life is not so ordinary; there are many exceptional moments, where God is in life. (Margaret Guenther)

Our teachers started each session with different forms of prayer. We read articles about listening, discernment, the importance of culture and traditions, spiritual development and healing. We wrote papers to help us see ourselves and others. We shared with the men and women of our group (about twenty) from all flavours of churches, varied ages and stages of life and spiritual growth. It was made clear the program was a process of discernment; not just taking a class and passing. The entire content fed, prodded and formed me. I loved it.

In the second year, we studied the Spiritual Exercises of St Ignatius (which each of us had participated in prior to acceptance to the program). As I said earlier, the Spiritual Exercises involve praying with certain scriptures, using all our senses and journaling. The scriptures are about the life of Jesus, and walking in our own lives, while in scripture. The exercises facilitate our paying attention to God in our ordinary lives.

In the third year, we practised spiritual direction with direct supervision. We wrote reflection papers after providing spiritual direction to pay attention to what movement (or energy I call it) we felt from the directee (companion). We wrote what we, ourselves, felt. The purpose of spiritual direction supervision is attentive listening to our own path with the directee to prevent an unconscious agenda from our own life. The spiritual director doesn't want her/his own life, or our own spiritual journey, to get in the way of the birthing, midwife of the soul, of the directee.

It took me three more years to meet the requirements of providing a hundred hours of spiritual direction, and seventy-five hours of supervision before I was certified.

I learned another spiritual director had contributed to my Cenacle education expense. I don't know how it all came about, but am eternally grateful and since then, I've been able to contribute to the Cenacle.

○

Early Life-Forming Memories.

During counselling and spiritual direction, early and mid-life, life-forming memories were shared. The memories now enlightened where I felt close to God, away from God, or abandoned by God. I was born in Kapuskasing, Ontario, Canada. Mum and Dad were married four years before I was born. Mum told me I was hard labour and delivery. One thing I imagine was hard and took away the joy of pregnancy was women in Mum's time weren't allowed to teach school if they were pregnant. The social norm was pregnant women wore loose clothing so visual signs of pregnancy were subdued. Mum was an elementary school teacher. She hid her pregnancy until shortly before I was born in May.

We moved to Terrace Bay, Ontario, Canada in 1949 when I was five years old. Terrace Bay, started in 1947, was a new paper mill town on the north shore of Lake Superior. Our first home was one of about forty homes. Dad was a chemical engineer at the paper mill.

Dad took me to the paper mill to show me his work.

As we drove up, I saw the large, two-story, light grey building set in an empty space. It was surrounded by evergreens. The building had a long tunnel-like projection from one wall. White smoke flowed into the clouds from the chimney.

Once in the paper mill building, Dad held my hand as we climbed stairs to a dining hall. The dining hall was inviting with its permeating smell of cookies baking and twelve long tables with separate sturdy chairs. At each table there were one or two strong-looking men sitting, drinking coffee or tea in mugs. Each man had a cookie, as large as the palm of my dad's hand. I'd never seen anything like it. The men smiled and asked me if I'd like a cookie. I did. Dad had one too. They were warm peanut butter cookies. I saw men baking in the connected kitchen. When we finished our cookies, Dad and I stood and looked out the window at the river many feet below us. The reflecting dark river water was filled with light-brown logs, the trunks of trees. Balanced on top of the logs were men dressed in one-piece brown suits. Each man had a long dangerous looking logging pike in his hand. The men worked swiftly, balancing themselves on the logs rolling under their feet; moving the logs with their sharp pike toward the mouth of the jack-ladder. The steep upward-moving rows of the metal jack-ladder took the logs to a protected area we couldn't see, where the logs were cut into chips. Dad said the wood chips were cooked. He said the product created our writing paper.

○

Around age six, I hiked into the tree-covered hills behind the elementary school. The sun shone on my feet as I ascended the lightly worn path of damp sand and rocks. Nature beckoned gently with the wind's freedom. It touched my face. It whispered delight in my hair. At the top of the hill, I discovered a large grey rock, a third my size. The rock's sides felt smooth, with flat spaces on top. It had black spots and sparkling silver flecks. I lifted pieces of moist, green, moss from the damp ground and carefully placed the finely woven roots on flat spaces. I added clusters of the green-leafed plants with red berries that grew amid the moss. My eyes received my creation's relevance. It was my altar; a gift for God.

As I stood up. I looked into the spaces between the brush and young trees. I yearned to meet God. I yearned to know I belonged. I stood taller, to survey the rest of my surreal surroundings. I saw magnificent Lake Superior in the distance. I felt a sense of wonder. It was for God and me.

○

My sister was born in a Quonset hut shortly after we moved to Terrace Bay. When older, we played outside in our fenced-in backyard. In June, it got warm enough to play outside without a jacket; however, the minuscule black flies tortured us, biting at the base of our hair and on our faces. They left itchy scabs. Mum put nylon stockings over our heads to protect us. The nylon stockings weren't comfortable and made us look funny with flat noses.

Mum took a clean bed sheet and laid it on our living room carpet in the warm sun. She took our favoured beige and black leather hassock we sometimes played with and set it in the middle of the sheet. She brought a plate of enticing meat and lettuce sandwiches, sweet homemade pickles and cookies and set them on the hassock. Mum, my sister and I sat on the clean sheet around the hassock. The three of us relished our peaceful, bug-free indoor picnic in the sun's warm glow. It was a once in a lifetime treasured oasis with my mum.

○

In midwinter, our Brownie meeting (Brownies are part of Girl Guides of Canada and Girl Scouts of United States of America), was held in the bright high school auditorium. We girls of seven and eight years old sat under imitation toadstools on imitation green grass. We were told what we needed to do to become a full-fledged Brownie. Our triple-folded Brownie card indicated one expectation was how to make and serve a proper cup of tea.

Learning the ritual of making tea played an important role in my whole life, and certainly when I became aware of a life of reflection. No matter how good or how hard the news, first, the tea kettle was put on the stove. The kettle was heated to bring cold water to hot, just this side of boiling. Hot water was added to the Brown Betty Teapot, or other colourful painted china teapot, to pre-warm the pot. The black tea leaves were carefully chosen and measured into the infuser. The water warming the pot was discarded. The infuser was put into the teapot and hot water was added. The teapot was covered with a hand-knit tea cosy. Then, with both hands, the covered teapot was patted with affection and faith it would brew a sacramental tea to uphold the spirit.

I left my Brownie meeting to walk the short distance home. My boots crunched with each step in the crisp shin-deep snow. My warm breath created a frozen pattern on the wool scarf across my mouth. Though it was suppertime, it was dark except for the dim streetlight I left at school and the one near home. I stopped and leaned back to look at the surrounding darkness. I yearned to see the stars. The deep black sky was alive with dancing bands of yellow, green and pink light. The bands moved constantly, changing, yet stayed in formation. The dancing-coloured energy drew my breath away, and then returned it, bringing awe...the breath of life. *It was God.*

When I got home, I told my parents what I'd seen. They said it was the northern lights, the Aurora Borealis. I never told them I knew it was God. (Cogger)

○

Before we had a piano, my mum arranged weekly piano lessons with a nun at a Roman Catholic convent in Schreiber, fifteen miles west of Terrace Bay. This meant Mum drove thirty miles round-trip every week in wild country with no phones, on gravel roads, and no gas station along the way. She waited for me in the car outside the convent. She'd also arranged for me to routinely practice on a neighbour's piano. (My mum played the piano and the organ in church for years as a young woman. She was able to play by ear, too)

I was unprepared, frightened and fascinated with the unknown world of the convent. The convent was a two-story wood-frame house with an entry that led to glass doors. The doors closed when I entered the small wood-scented parlour. The room contained an upright piano and a high-backed wood chair that squeaked when my instructor sat down. My instructor, Sister Irene, had a pleasant, soft-looking face with silver-rimmed glasses, surrounded in white cloth with a white cloth strap under her chin. It looked tight. She wore a long black dress along with black shoes.

In the convent entry, there was a flight of stairs. Each stair squeaked as a nun went upstairs during my lessons; to where I wondered? The convent and my instructor, who I saw as a mysterious person with an intriguing life, were far more interesting to me than the piano lessons.

I asked questions about the convent and nuns on the way home; nothing about the lesson. Mum said the nuns cut their hair short and wore the white head covering, called a habit, and the long dark clothes as part of their religion. I never thought to ask more about their life.

I found practising the piano pieces arduous, first at our neighbour's home where I reluctantly entered to try my unsure fingers, and then at home when we got a beautiful piano. When I practised, Mum called from the other room, "Ugh, ugh, try again. Nope, nope, try again."

○

Mr and Mrs Smith lived next door to us in our second home in Terrace Bay. Mrs Smith was my first-grade teacher. She had to leave our class for many weeks to have surgery. My mum became our teacher. My mum had gone to a teacher's college in North Bay, Ontario. She had taught in a country school before she married, sometimes children in many grades, in one room.

On the first day my mum became my first-grade teacher, I talked without being called upon. In a stern tone, my mum promptly told me it wasn't acceptable. I was embarrassed and was quiet. When home, Mum told me, "I can't show any favouritism. You have to set a good example." Indeed, from then on, I set a good example.

After many weeks, Mum wasn't our teacher anymore. I was glad Mrs Smith returned. I liked her. I wasn't afraid of her. We learned how to write, with an eraser on our wrist to keep it straight. I was good at printing; however, my writing didn't slant correctly. I knew perfect handwriting was important to my mum.

In third grade, we had a new Principal, his wife, their daughter, who was my age, and a son, six years old, who lived in the home the Smiths had lived in, next door to us. The girl my age was tall and thin with black curly hair like her father. She was quick to move and spoke loudly.

Next to our elementary school was an outdoor skating rink surrounded by wood boards. I wanted to play hockey but girls weren't allowed to play hockey. We did get to free-skate and slide on the ice.

Soon after my neighbour girl moved into the house next door, she wouldn't let me on the ice rink, though she let other schoolmates in. Her physical demeanour, with a threatening face, kept me off. While playing near the rink, her maroon wool hat blew off. The second I saw the hat leave her head; I ran. I grabbed her hat and threw it up onto the one-story, snow-covered school roof. It landed two feet beyond the roof's edge. At that moment, I knew that was trouble. I went home. The vision of the hat on the roof didn't sit well with me. I couldn't stop thinking about it. I kept it to myself.

The next day, I was called to the Principal's office to see her father, our principal. I walked down the light green shiny hall. My shoes made enough sound for others to know I was walking to the principal's office. Our principal's tall thin body loomed largely. He asked me to sit in the wooden chair across from his desk. He asked me why I threw a student's, and his daughter's hat on the school roof. I said, "She wouldn't let me on the rink." I didn't cry. I didn't feel. I just was. If he said anymore, I didn't hear him. He let me go. Going back to class, seeing faces, saying nothing, I resumed class as though nothing had happened. When home, I was afraid of what Mum and Dad would do when they found out. There were always consequences, no matter the reason. Mum always asked what other people would say. I never heard another word from anyone.

◯

Christmas was coming. Dad took my sister and me in the car to get our Christmas tree. He brought along an axe and wood toboggan. We drove a short while, eager to see the desired out of town spruce trees. We both had on snowsuits, winter boots, hats and mitts. No sunglasses for any of us. Our eyes blinked in the glare of the sun reflecting from the pure white knee-deep snow.

We walked a short distance on the snow-covered road. We couldn't see our breath today. Dad instructed us to get on the toboggan. He pulled with all his strength to get us up the snow bank to the soft layer of snow. He was now walking in knee-deep snow with his high boots, warm jacket and leather-lined gloves. He wore his warm hat with the fur flaps, but today he didn't need them over his ears. He trudged along with steady strength, his heels sending a spray of snowflakes containing eagerness and joy. He asked us to look for our Christmas tree. It was to be as tall as he, to have a lovely shape for ornaments and the tree-top angel. As he moved along, we pointed to this one and that one. We loved the ride.

He stopped. He measured himself beside the tree and put his hand up to the top. He asked us what we thought. We simultaneously nodded our heads with a "yes". We got off the toboggan, laughing as we manoeuvred our bodies in the deep snow. Dad took his axe, and first, kneeled in the snow to cut limbs from the bottom. He playfully threw them at us. He again stood and leaned over, swinging his axe at the base of the tree trunk. Again and again, his strength made its way on one side, then the other. He prepared us for the tree toppling with "Tim…ber!"

We sat on the toboggan sitting together as close as possible. He placed the treasured prickly tree in our laps to hold while returning to the car. The scent of the boughs and sap invigorated our sense of the season and brought deep inhales of satisfaction. Once home, we watched as Dad trimmed the end of the tree trunk with a saw so it would stand tall and straight in the stand. Mum took the boughs from the bottom of the tree to decorate our dining room table. Dad stood the tree up in a bucket of water in the dining room to let the tree thaw and drink before he put it in the Christmas tree stand to be decorated the next day.

Dad brought boxes of lights and decorations from the basement. He and Mum worked to get the tree in the right place in the living room. They worked to get it upright, straight and anchored in the stand. He put water in the stand and said I needed to check the water level every day to see if the tree needed more water. I felt grown up. The strings of lights were laid on the living room floor and plugged in to make sure the series of lights worked. A dead bulb had to be changed. We had a couple of extra bulbs in the boxes.

As Mum watched, Dad strung the lights from top to bottom going around the tree. The angel had to be at the top where the strings started. Mum told Dad to move the strings as he went along, sometimes he had to undo and start again. Again, and again, Mum had Dad re-do an area so it was right.

Their voices got louder and faster with each exchange. I shrank. Dad left the room.

Mum moved strings around. She opened the boxes of beautiful, coloured ornaments. We could look but not touch. She looked carefully and decided where each ornament should go, sometimes repositioning it. When all the ornaments were secured, she started with silver foil tinsel. The tinsel lay in straight bands in the secured box. Only Mum could put the tinsel on each branch, putting on one long strand at a time. One end was looped over the branch and allowed to fall into a long icicle-like form with many on each branch. It took her a long time. I wanted to decorate but couldn't and wouldn't dare ask. I left until she finished, then returned to admire the tree, with lights flickering in my mind.

○

Christmas Eve, my sister and I, with Mum and Dad's help, put a plate on the kitchen table with homemade Christmas cookies and a glass of milk for Santa. Dad gave us fresh carrots with their green feathery leaves for the reindeer. He wrote our note to Santa saying, "Thank you for coming. Help yourself to cookies." We were willing to go to bed early so Santa would come. We each found a big sock, one of Dad's clean socks, and pinned it to the ends of our twin beds. Our slippers, dressing gowns, and hairbrush were readied for the morning.

I awakened while it was dark and my sister still sleeping. I felt for my sock, misshapen, heavy and full. My heart was excited; my mind trying to guess what was in my sock as I felt the outside of it. I got up, unpinned it from the bedspread and laid it on the bed. While sitting on the bed, gently and quietly, I pulled out and examined each item in the early morning twilight. I felt a smooth shiny barrette. Then FIVE gold, foil-covered chocolate coins. I remembered the same thing from last year that looked like gold money and tasted of velvety smooth chocolate. I knew I had to wait to open any, but imagined the coming flavour. Next came many shapes of nuts we would crack. I thought I would be able to handle the nut-cracker myself this year. Next, I could tell by the size and feel that it was a big red pomegranate. What a treasure that was. It was rare to see and we only had them at Christmas time. I loved the tangy brilliant red seeds. Lastly, a tangerine emerged from the sock toe. I passed my hands back and forth over my gifts, savouring them in the dark. I carefully put them back in the sock, laid down with them in my arms to rest and wait for the rest of the family to awaken.

Finally, Mum and Dad got up when they heard me and my sister talking. They stood and listened in our doorway as we each exclaimed and showed our stocking contents. Mum helped us put on our dressing gowns and made sure our hair was brushed. My sister and I just wanted to get to the Christmas tree. Dad called from the bottom of the stairs we could come down. As we entered the stairs, bright floodlights from a metal beam Dad was holding glared at us, forcing me to hang my head. For the journey downstairs, I forgot Christmas.

We stopped at the stair bottom and saw the tree. I stood and breathed in. There were many colourful packages under the tree, and there were two dolls, one with a small crib, and one with a highchair. We looked at Mum to see if we could go to the tree and toys. She nodded. We both held a doll and tried out the crib and high chair. There was a crib blanket, sheet and pillow, hand-made. There were bibs with the high chair. Finally, Dad turned off the floodlights.

We took turns carefully opening packages, one at a time, saving the precious wrapping paper Mum refolded and put in a pile. My sister and I got soft long robes. The tree lights were left on all day.

When finished with the packages, we eagerly went to the kitchen and saw the partly eaten carrots and scattered carrot tops, some cookie crumbs and an empty glass of milk. Yep, Santa had come and brought us our dolls, high chair and crib, and Rudolph the reindeer had left a mess.

○

We visited my grandparents by making an annual summer car trip. There were infrequently sent long-hand letters from my parents to each of their parents. "To stay in touch," my dad said. There weren't letters from grandparents to their grandchildren, as I have done and do with my own grandchildren. No internet was available in the 1950s and '60s. We didn't have superhighways with gas stations or restaurants near the highways.

Let me tell you about one trip we made, enjoying the journey with a couple of stops, rather than just focusing on the destination.

We normally travelled from morning till night in the heat of summer (no car air conditioners) with a metal thermos of water, packed sandwiches and a few books. We travelled from Terrace Bay to North Bay, Ontario, first, to see my maternal grandmother.

For entertainment on the two-lane highways surrounded by trees, we watched for deer, moose, and birds. It was thrilling to see deer, and even more so the rare moose standing in a pond of lily pads. If we were in an area where we saw many cars, we pointed out license plates, hoping for more than an Ontario license. Otherwise, we were to be quiet, sometimes reinforced with a barking threat from my dad. We couldn't open the windows because it would mess up Mum's hair.

On this trip, we stopped for an hour at Niagara Falls, the Ontario side. It was a sunny warm day. People of all ages were dressed in colourful summer clothes and gathered around the decorative black metal fencing to protect us while gazing at the falls. The power of the vast amount of fresh-water falling created a rushing noise and white foam on the surface of quieter water below. The turbulence lifted mist into the air we gleefully enjoyed it on our faces. I deeply inhaled. Below, we saw the Maid of the Mist boat. The boat was full of passengers. It went close to the misty falls far below us. It looked exciting. I wished we could go.

We stopped at a nearby peach orchard, our first and only experience in an orchard. The peach trees stood in straight rows with green leaves and yellow-pink skins of the peaches hanging amid the leaves. With Dad's lifting help, my sister and I picked our own peaches. We gently polished them on our clothes to make sure they were clean and took a bite. The juice of my peach ran down my chin, caught by my finger, swiping it up into my mouth before Mum's white handkerchief caught it. The peach was sweet, like tasting sunshine. I yearned to run amid the trees and exclaim freedom…but no, not today.

Mum's (my mum's mother) three-story brick and wood house in North Bay had six white painted wooden steps to an expansive front porch with white wood railings. The porch was flanked by green-leafed bushes with mixing-bowl sized white scented flowers. The porch landing was where I first saw my maternal grandfather. He was in a wooden, high-backed rocking chair with arms. Without moving his head, his eyes turned toward us. He looked at us but didn't speak or smile. He sat upright, with no facial expression. He was a tall, lean man with grey hair. Without any touch or word, Mum walked past him. My mum, in the past, said her father and her uncle, Dick, loved Christmas and were funny.

I never saw my grandmother care for my grandfather. He was clean, with a white shirt unbuttoned at the neck and long sleeves with beige trousers. He slept upstairs with Mum, but I never saw him walk. Maybe one of her two men borders helped her when moving him. It was never mentioned. In our entire family, my parents and their parents included, pride and dignity were paramount. A person couldn't appear needy or appear not being proper. Maybe it was the English background infused into Canadian culture.

Mum's home entrance was filled with daylight and with a carpeted stairway to the second-floor bedrooms. The formal living room to the right looked inviting, yet untouchable, with a stuffed rose-coloured soft couch and chair, a wood end table and a tall lamp.

From the front entry, the large kitchen was straight ahead. Before the kitchen, there was a white painted door on the left to the grey stone basement. In the basement, Mum had a washer that sloshed the clothes around, and a wringer to squeeze the water from the dripping clothes. I watched Mum carefully put the wet clothes through the wringer, one at a time without getting fingers pinched. She let me put one piece through. The clothes were taken in a large woven basket to the backyard and hung to dry on a clothesline. Mum's ironing was done in the bright airy kitchen on a standing covered board with a heavy, black-handled iron. I silently watched her. Mum wasn't unfriendly. I think she was always thinking about what she had to do next with the house, garden, my grandfather, and borders. Once, she asked me what was wrong with my mum. I looked at my grandmother, puzzled, and said I didn't know.

Mum baked and cooked every day, every meal. I LOVED her two-inch-high baking powder and brown sugar biscuits with giant raisins, especially when dripping with the butter she applied for our first bite. One of her borders worked for the department of agriculture and brought her butter samples. Mum told me she had boarders living with her to support herself and her children (my mum, her younger sister and younger brother). "So they could get an education." My grandfather was much older than her. He'd come to Canada from India. He was one of eleven boys. His father was in the British military in India. According to my mum, her dad wanted to be a gentleman farmer but that didn't work out. My grandmother had an eighth-grade education. She came from a blended family of eleven children.

The house's second floor had a bathroom (the only bathroom) with a claw foot white ceramic tub, toilet, sink, and a straight wood chair. There was still lots of space. I watched Mum from her bedroom doorway as she sat on the satin-cushioned stool at her dressing table. She opened a silver round box, took the powder puff, dipped it in the light pink powder and patted it across her attractive face of lines and brown spots. She brushed her greying, short curly hair away from her face and upward. When home, Mum wore a short-sleeved print cotton dress and low-heeled shoes. When outside, she added a broad-brimmed hat. When she worked in her backyard garden she whistled, no particular tune. Viewing her happy in her hat with a whistle in her garden was a lovely sight. Maybe that's why I love hats.

Mum brought orange carrots with long leafy green tops and green-topped onions from her garden for our dinner. She wore a printed apron that covered all of her, tied in the back. Her pressure cooker exploded in the kitchen sending its brown and green contents to the ceiling, some dripping to the tile floor. No one was in the kitchen at the moment. Mum got a ladder to clean it up and Dad helped her. Mum got a bucket of water and old towels. Dad wiped the ceiling in a circular fashion. Mum rinsed the towels and sent them back up the wooden ladder to Dad. They smiled and laughed when the mess started to clear. I was relieved and happy to see their mutual responses.

The boarders stayed in the two small bedrooms across from the master bedroom and the one and only bathroom. My sister and I slept in the third-floor double bed. The third floor was entered through a white painted door and up the linoleum covered narrow, steep staircase. The very warm room at the top had windows that overlooked the street. On rare occasions, my sister and I slid down the staircase bumping our feet onto the closed door. It only lasted for one ride before we were chastised, but it was worth one trip.

A chubby, favoured joyful man of my mum's age lived a few blocks away. We visited him and he took all of us in his car to Lake Nipissing. The lake looked vast extending from a sandy beach to the blue sky. It was shallow. We got to play (except Mum who couldn't swim) in the warm lake staying within the stated boundaries. It was a rare treat to have freedom and fun.

Mum often spoke in an angry voice to Mum. That always shocked me because I was terrified to ever "talk back" to Mum or Dad. When my mum expressed angry words, my grandmother kept doing what she wanted to be done, hardly responding to Mum. Dad stayed out of the way. Mum often complained that growing up, her younger sister didn't appreciate material things and got away with a lot. Mum's material possessions were very important to her.

We stayed with Mum for a few days, then travelled to Toronto to see Dad's family. They lived on Durie St, (near Dundas St where we caught the streetcar to downtown Toronto). Grandpa and Grandma had a two-story red brick home. They had a one-car garage entered from the alley at the end of the backyard. Grandpa had many locks on the inside of the light green back door of the house. From the front door of the house, the entry was small, dark, and carpeted with wooden stairs straight ahead. The small parlour to the right, entered through two glass doors had a velvet dark-red couch and chairs. The second set of parlour doors opened to a spacious wallpapered dining room with heavy wood furniture.

During a meal, Grandma sat at one end and Grandpa at the other end of the table. Grandma never spoke a word to us, ever. She was on the heavy side with a large nose that was a little red. She passed the dishes, and seemed fine, but didn't talk with us. Grandma's quiet always puzzled me. When I asked Mum about Grandma's silence, she dryly said, "Grandma always thought I wasn't good enough for your dad."

Aunt Evelyn lived there too. She was Dad's oldest sister who took a streetcar every workday to her job as an executive secretary at Eaton's in downtown Toronto. When we came,

Aunt Evelyn slept in the downstairs parlour so my sister and I could have her double bed off the only bathroom at the top of the stairs.

The downstairs large bright kitchen had a round white painted table in the centre of the tile floor, halfway between the sink and the stove.

Grandpa was a railroad engineer for fifty years. He was gone a lot. According to my paternal cousin, Grandma was a kind woman who helped neighbouring women, was active in the Baptist Church, and cared for my Uncle Jim. As a child, Uncle Jim was ill with an open wound on his leg caused by a bone disease. More than one doctor predicted he would lose his leg. Grandma nursed him back to health. This view of Grandma was totally foreign to me.

When at their house, I loved awakening in the early morning quiet. I went to Mum and Dad's room next door to ours. Mom and I whispered so we wouldn't awaken anyone else. Mom opened our suitcase, laid out my clothes and indicated I needed to get dressed. I brushed my light-brown long curls and put on my plaid dress and patent shoes with white socks. I carefully descended the dark stairs, eager to see Grandpa stir the cup of bubbly soap that looked like white frosting, and brush it on his face. I could hear the slapping sound, then the dragging of the straight razor on the leather strap from the kitchen. Entering the kitchen was like entering another house. The sun shone through the sheer white curtains onto the grey tile floor. The silver metal kettle simmered on the large wood stove. The fresh scent of soap and water beckoned.

I entered without a word and saw Grandpa near the sink. His razor strap hung from a silver rack in the near corner. A small mirror big enough for him to examine his chin hung from the wall. Grandpa's thin grey hair was neatly parted and combed in place. He had on a dressy plaid wool shirt and wool vest with khaki-coloured trousers, clean with a severe crease. I loved to be with Grandpa though there was never much conversation and certainly not while he was shaving.

Grandpa was kind and welcoming with his voice and smile. There was no physical demonstration of affection. I was fascinated as Grandpa tightened his face with a finger from one hand and guided the straight razor through the white soapsuds to give way to pink smooth skin. He didn't turn but was aware I was watching. I had a sense he had many thoughts wanting to know me better. I would have loved to have leapt into his arms, hugged him and laughed aloud, but it was not proper, and I had to be proper. When only traces of the white foam were left at the base of his nostrils and ears, he took a fresh white linen towel and wiped his face. He then turned and said, "We'll go to Terra's Cottage today for lunch. We'll stop and buy meat pies to bring home. Do you like meat pies?"

○

Terrace Bay had a Roman Catholic Church and a Protestant Community Church. The Community Church was our church. Mum and we children attended routinely. Our minister, Reverend Lavender, a somewhat portly, sweet man who on rare occasions came to our home for dinner with his wife.

My mum never talked about God. We never said prayers; however, she insisted we dress appropriately to attend our Community Church. She made it clear we must behave. Displaying impeccable manners, dressing appropriately, and being seen and not heard were the givens of life. Life was based on what should be done, often with Mum's right index finger pointed at my eye with her hostile glare behind it.

At this time in life, God was a male figure above me, supreme and I tried to please God.

I was asked to be Mary, mother of Christ, in the Christmas church play. Mum helped me memorise what I was to do, when, and how to say my line. I sat on a stool at the front of the congregation as a reader told the story of an angel coming to Mary and telling her she would have a baby. In the story, Mary said, "She pondered these things in her heart." (America) (Luke2:19) The word pondered took up residence in my heart with a question mark.

When the reader nodded at me, I said, "I'm going to have a son and his name is Jesus." (America)(Luke 1:31) I was dressed in a long plain white dress with a blue head-dress that surrounded my face and hung to my shoulders. I was given the baby Jesus (a doll wrapped in a blanket), and continued to sit and hold him. A boy dressed in a white long dress with a brown jacket holding a tall cane was with me. Other children dressed as shepherds and wise men came to see Jesus as our parents sang.

○

Mum took me with her to the Anglican Church in the next town of Schreiber fifteen miles from Terrace Bay. Attending the church in Schreiber was special to her. It was a rare occurrence.

I loved the quaint church too. I loved its wood carvings, its altar with many candles, and its wooden pews. The church was gleaming with candlelight. The candles emitted a waxy scent. Each person was dressed up, men in suits and women in dresses with hats. Wearing a hat was an expectation of women while in the Anglican Church. I followed along as we stood and sang, kneeled on kneelers and prayed, sat and listened. Mostly, I looked around taking in the colours of stained-glass windows.

After the service, a lady who looked older than Mum, who Mum knew, asked us to come to her house for tea. Mum introduced Mrs Bailey and me and gladly accepted her invitation. We sat at a round wooden table draped with a white tablecloth. The table was just big enough for the three of us. It had a small vase with a flower from Mrs Bailey's large, gorgeous garden I saw when we walked to her front door. Mrs Bailey brought a teapot that was white china with a bouquet of flowers painted on it. Her sugar bowl, cream pitcher, cups and saucers all matched the teapot. We had white linen serviettes (napkins). I opened mine, placing it on my lap as Mum did. Mrs Bailey brought a tray with butter knives, small plates, and a plate of warm scones. Next, she brought a glass dish of butter and a small jar of raspberry jam, with a little spoon. She said she had made the jam from last year's berries. I smiled inside and out. Mum and Mrs Bailey talked and talked. I was happy enjoying my demitasse cup of tea with milk and sugar and a scone with raspberry jam. I hoped we could come again.

O

Dad's parents and Dad's oldest sister, Aunt Evelyn came from Toronto, Ontario, to our home once, while we lived in Terrace Bay. Aunt Evelyn brought me a Golden Book. It was about Jesus. The cover had a picture of Jesus with children around him. Aunt Evelyn invited me to sit on her lap while she read it to me. While she read, I felt warmth rise from her lap into my body. The tender warmth with a kind voice was a new lovely experience.

When Aunt Evelyn wasn't around, my parents talked and laughed about her, ridiculing her interest in church and Jesus.

When we travelled as a family to Toronto, Canada, to visit Dad's parents, Aunt Evelyn once took me to her Baptist Church. We witnessed a full immersion baptism. I was fascinated. I wondered if water ran down the minister's arms when he passionately preached after the immersion. He held his hands high in the air as he exclaimed the importance of baptism and Jesus. I knew I'd been baptised in the Anglican Church as an infant in Kapuskasing, Ontario. I was aware of the specialness of the church. God, for me, just was and Jesus, a picture book image.

○

On a blue-sky day, Dad and I drove for miles on gravel roads to a forest path marked with a tall wooden stake. Dad got out of the car, let me out and put on his backpack. I had on long pants, a long-sleeved t-shirt, and my old shoes. He started walking ahead of me on the narrow earthen path. His hand beckoned me to follow. The path quickly entered the dark forest with rays of sunlight amid the spruce and pine trees. From the earth to Dad's waist was a thick bush on both sides of the path. I walked briskly on the five-mile hike mimicking Dad's movements to keep up. We walked up slippery hills of sand and rocks hanging onto branches pulling ourselves up and held on going down. Dad held onto or broke branches fierce enough to snap behind him into my eager attentive nine-year-old face. I sprawled and crawled one leg at a time over the rough bark of large fallen logs. I scrambled under thick brush. My breathing kept pace with my excitement.

Dad didn't speak. His body moved evenly with strength. I felt his zeal, his quiet acceptance of me, even appreciation. We paused beside a crystal clear rapidly flowing stream. It was so clear the grey rocks saluted hello from the bubbling water. He lifted the clear, cold water in his cupped hand to my thirsty mouth. I slurped from the loving cup. I can still see Dad's hand; large, firm, and full, with an iron ring made with octagonal shapes on his little finger (an engineer's ring that promises quality work). Dad and I watched for moose, grouse and rabbits. As our path approached the dark lake that reflected bright sun, I could see a cabin built of hand-hewn logs with small spaces between the logs. There weren't any other cabins or anyone else around. Dad removed a pad-lock and pushed open the heavy wooden door to a large, open space with a huge iron stove, wood table and stools. There were two stacks of three wood bunk beds attached to one long wall. The cabin smelled like the woods. Dad dropped his pack and got our fishing rods.

He helped me step into the green wooden canoe. I sat in the middle facing forward. We paddled. Dad showed me how to hold my paddle alongside the canoe. I concentrated on inserting and lifting my paddle with effective quiet. My first voyage.

Upon portaging to another lake, Dad stopped and kneeled on the ground beside the canoe with the canoe on its side. His strong body lifted the canoe onto his shoulders with the paddles held inside the canoe. I, in the fascination of this wonderland with Dad, carried the fishing poles keeping them straight ahead so they didn't get tangled in the bush. He pointed out the moccasin-shaped pink Lady Slippers. He told me not to pick them as they take seven years to bloom. Once we were on a dark reflecting lake again, Dad fixed our fishing poles with worms on the hooks. For a while, we sat in quiet looking around at the tree-lined lake. With an inner smile, I put my investigating fingers in the cold water. Dad's rod bent. We both laughed. I was amazed. He exclaimed, "We've got one, we've got one!" He caught a speckled trout, big enough to keep. It had a pink speckled belly. He left the trout in the cold water in a live net after we tied up the canoe for the night. He said we'd eat it when we had other fish tomorrow.

We were hungry! Dad fixed canned Franco-American Spaghetti with parmesan cheese for supper. He told me how the men worked to cut the logs, move them, and cut them to fit like a puzzle. He said our friend, Runi Ostling carried in the iron stove on his back. I read words in the book they kept of memories of, who came, how many fish they caught, and other sightings, like of moose. Wonder and joy were abundant, even about the two-hole wooden seat secured over a strong tree branch to serve as an outhouse. I was not moved to use it.

○

When I was nine years old and my sister was four years old, my dad taught us a fire escape plan. He told us the plan was in case we were alone on the second floor and couldn't safely use the stairs to get to a door and out of the house. Our bathroom was located at the top of the stairs with its window facing the front of our two-story house. He explained we were to take my child-size maple rocker with the sharp edges and slam it hard against the bathroom window, breaking it. Outside the bathroom window, three feet below it was a decorative two-foot-wide ledge across the front of the house. Dad explained that after the window was broken, we were to pad the window with bathroom towels. Then we were to, one at a time, carefully crawl out the window and stand on the wooden ledge and we would be rescued.

On a hot August day, Dad said he had to leave us a while. He said he would be back soon with my maternal grandmother. She had travelled from North Bay, to help while Mum was in the hospital. Mum was at the hospital with our new baby brother.

Since my sister and I were now alone, I felt highly responsible. I decided we needed to practise the fire escape plan. My sister and I dragged my child's rocker from our bedroom to the bathroom. In talking about our next step, since there was no fire, we decided we wouldn't break the window. With grunts of pulling and pushing with our young arms and fingers, we struggled to raise the window. We took soft green bathroom towels and laid them on the windowsill. I decided my sister needed to go out the window first because she needed a boost. I figured I would follow behind her with my longer, stronger legs. As I worked to keep my two-handed boost under my sister's thighs, she got her eager four-year-old legs up and over the sill, and slid down, to the waiting ledge. She looked back with a wide smile of accomplishment under her wispy blond hair. Just then, my dad pulled into the driveway with my grandmother. He looked up and opened his car door. He ran to the grassy area many feet below my sister. He stopped. He breathed. He told me to stay where I was. *Shucks!* I thought. As he looked at my little sister, he extended his strong arms upward and said, "I want you to…" Without a moment's hesitation, my happy sister jumped into his arms.

The next day, Dad took my sister and me to the newly built one-story McCausland Hospital, named after our one and only doctor. He lifted each of us, one at a time, high enough so we could see Mum sitting in bed with our baby brother. I was excited. Without words, I decided he was mine.

○

We emigrated from Canada to the United State in June of 1955. We went through Immigration Services in Toronto, Ontario. It was hot. The buildings were not air-conditioned. I was eleven years old, my sister was seven years old, and my brother was two years old. It took many hours. It seemed endless. Dad was in a suit and tie, Mum in a dress-up dress with stockings and high heels, my sister and I in dresses with dress shoes and socks and my brother in a button-down shirt with matching shorts with button-down straps and his white shoes and socks. My brother wanted to run around. There weren't any toys or books or snacks. We had to be on our best behaviour to meet with the authorities and get our green immigration cards to live in the United States. Dad had to go into the office alone first. When he came out, he told Mum he was asked questions and had a physical exam. He talked in whispers.

We received our green immigration cards.

○

As soon as we arrived at our destination in Neenah, Wisconsin, we went to Mrs Heartl's home. Dad had stayed with Mrs Heartl while he started his new job at Kimberly Clark Corporation. He found a house he and Mum liked and made arrangements for us to come.

Mrs Heartl had short, thin white hair. Her face had many brown spots. She had flesh that hung from under her chin. Her smile was broad, her laugh inviting as she asked us to enter her home. The doorway entered lots of space with a few chairs. A dining room table was surrounded by more chairs. My brother was able to walk around. Mrs Heartl didn't care.

She immediately asked us to sit at the dining room table covered with a beige tablecloth of needlework. The house smelled of tantalising food. All of us were extremely hungry. She brought a platter of fried chicken, a bowl of mashed potatoes, a gravy boat filled to the brim, and a bowl of honey-covered carrots. *Yum*, I thought. Oh, how we enjoyed her meal and her hospitality.

Afterwards, Mrs Heartl invited me to a card table with play cards. She started to teach me how to play Canasta. I understood and liked it. She was sweet, friendly, and laughed. I could tell she loved Dad and he loved her. Mrs Heartl said she was glad to meet us and would also miss our dad. In the months to come, we would visit her again.

○

Since we moved in the summer of 1955, during the polio epidemic, we couldn't leave our yard. One house on our block said, "Quarantined." Someone in the home had polio. We knew it was a serious infectious disease. We and all our neighbours took it seriously. Fortunately, we were able to go to school in the fall of 1955. The polio vaccine became available after years of research. The research scientist, Dr Salk, vaccinated his own son first to show the Salk Polio Vaccine was safe.

Though the polio epidemic (meaning the spread of infection was in a localised area) had been going on for a few years now, we were lucky we only had months of staying home, unlike the 2020 COVID-19 pandemic, (a larger population, USA and globally) I'll talk about later.

Newspapers and magazines showed pictures of people and children, who were paralysed from polio. An iron lung was created to help a person breathe, whose breathing muscles were affected, keeping them alive for years. (As a nurse, I observed care of a young woman with an iron lung around 1970).

We looked at neighbours' yards and watched for activity. At the dinner table, there'd be a comment about a person laying in the sun in their bathing suit, or how children were playing in the yard. I wondered what each person was like. Many times, there wasn't anyone to watch as people were in their homes or backyards. We did have a two-story home with three bedrooms, two bathrooms and a recreation room as well as living and dining rooms. We had a fenced-in yard and a garage.

Even if I could have left the yard in our new home, I missed an imagined place to hike or look for tadpoles in a stream. There was no nearby store where I could ride my bike and get a mint chocolate bar.

In Canada, I completed three grades in two years so I was a year younger than my seventh-grade peers. Initially, I wasn't able to join the United States Girl Scout meetings because I had to be twelve. When finally twelve the next spring, Mrs Kramer was my leader. We earned many badges while meeting in her home. My peers talked about wearing nylon stockings, applying lipstick, and going to dances. I felt a bizarre gap in life, the life I loved in nature.

○

Soon after we moved to Neenah, Dad travelled for two to three weeks at a time. He went to Chihuahua, Mexico where Kimberly Clark was building a new paper mill. There was no direct deposit of checks. People didn't make long-distance calls just to talk. Long-distance calling was expensive. Long-distance calling was only for emergencies. Mum had the care of us; three children, the house, groceries, cooking, paying bills, and making sure we did our homework. She barely knew any of our any neighbours on Hazel Street. Mum blamed Dad's boss for his long travels. She fed our feelings of abandonment by Dad and his work.

Mum was upset with a letter from Dad. In a huff of hurt, she said, "He only talks business." She was angry, actually rage-full. Her forceful body movements spoke of anger, her words were loud, sharp and sometimes a litany of disappointments and pain. Then she didn't speak for days. The silence was filled with seething resentment. I felt Mum's oozing hostility. It unpredictably spewed out like a venomous snake as she pointed her finger at me and said, "You make me…" Whatever it was, it was my fault. I shrank. My sister and I talked about calling Dad's boss and telling him to tell Dad to come home.

○

I stood on the elevated stage in my new white sweater Mum bought me, my pleated brown skirt above my 11-year-old knees, wearing my resented Buster Brown shoes. I wanted the newest soft saddle shoes my peers were wearing. I was overruled.

Before me was the vast slanted auditorium floor. The auditorium was filled with seventh and eighth-grade students seated in their flip-top desks. Numbness permeated me. I was speaking to new students and teachers and would be judged. Being judged was terrifying. What if I failed?

In my Kimberly Junior High School English class, our assignment was to pick a category of writing, write about our subject, and present it to our fellow students with the idea of winning in the category. When given the assignment I had no idea what category or subject to choose, how, or where to start.

I'd excelled in grade school; however, we were in a new city, and we'd been quarantined since we moved in June. I didn't know anyone. I'd never seen, let alone been in a two-story junior high school where we changed classes and classrooms. I hadn't been to the public library yet. Mostly I was terrified of the whole thing.

I was empty and felt frozen inside when I told my mum what I had to do. She said, "How about a serious oration talking about the United Nations?" I'd never heard of the United Nations (UN). I gladly took the subject because I had no ideas forming. Mum called me "impudent" if I said anything to contradict or question her.

I began my work by reading our encyclopaedias (many decades before the internet). I picked out what was important, brought the facts together, and told why I thought the UN was a good idea. I read and reread my creation to be able to speak well.

I took my creation to Mum for the homework approval she demanded to make sure it was right. With her long-fingered hands and her silence full of information, she crossed out and added words. I silently stood next to her hoping for her approval. Upon completion, she handed the speech back to me. Without words and with a straight face, she put her familiar right-hand fingers on my chest and gave me a push, meaning I could go. Actually, it was a command. The silent message was it was now acceptable; no discussion needed.

When I read my speech there was nothing left of mine. It wasn't my paper. The words weren't mine. It made me want to disappear, to be gone. I felt like crying but didn't. Mum would be furious and frightening. With my submerged fear of not presenting perfectly, I presented the serious oration.

After all the presentations, winners were called to the stage for each category. I was presented a medal for the serious oration by our Principal.

I smiled but felt awful. My smile was the usual smile I wore. I felt less. *I didn't deserve it. I didn't write it. It was a lie.*

○

After we moved to Neenah, Mum took me to St Thomas Episcopal Church (the Episcopal Church of the USA is similar to the Anglican Church). I started to attend youth group.

My dad never spoke of God. He detested religion. Mum attended St Thomas Church too, however, she didn't become involved in the church in other ways this time. When I was confirmed, Mum sewed me a white brocade dress I loved. I had new shoes for this occasion, red flats. They were delicious in looks and feel. Amazingly, Dad came. Confirmation was expected of me by Mum, but I also wanted to join. I had learned what I needed to learn from the Book of Common Prayer about God, Jesus, prayer and my commitment. I correctly answered questions by the bishop who confirmed us. It was an honour and humbling to me. I wanted to be an acolyte and light the altar candles. However, no girls were allowed to participate in anything at the altar in the Episcopal Church yet. I accepted it without a word, but yet another tuck of disappointment was added to not being able to play hockey as a girl.

Our youth group visited the Episcopal Diocese of Fond du Lac Convent, in Fond du Lac, Wisconsin. A young nun showed us her simple room with a bed, desk, chair and closet.

She told us she went to morning and evening vespers and worked within the convent between services. For the church service, the Episcopal priest was dressed in white vestments. He waved a gold-coloured incense vessel while processing into the church service. The haze of incense smoke travelled into each pew. I'd never experienced incense. The smoke was inviting, mysterious and made me cough. The altar candles glimmered. The organ music led to singing. It was unifying and majestic. I wondered if I'd like to be a nun. I didn't know the Episcopal Church had nuns.

I thought about God. I tried to please God. I strived to be perfect. It was what we were to do.

○

When Dad came home from out-of-town work trips, life was worse. The tension was high. I feared for my younger brother's safety because of my dad's impatience and my mum's vacillating protection and rejection of all of us. When Dad came home after three weeks away, my two-year-old brother took off on his tricycle before we realised he was gone from the backyard. I ran and found him. He was at the end of Hazel Street joining Cecil St, where he could have been hit by a car.

When Mum picked him up, he flailed his body, crying with anger. Mum and Dad were upset too. I realised my brother was jealous of my dad since my brother was usually alone with Mum until Dad came home. Mum resented Dad too because she had to run everything when he was gone. Though Dad wanted to help, everything shifted.

I saw Mum and Dad's body movements of reaching out and then retreating arms. It was a confusing time. There were never any explanations for what we children witnessed. Perhaps they were in private.

At times when Dad came home, Mum left for days without a word of warning or explanation. It was as though she had disappeared. Dad calmly cared for us fixing food and working in the garden. I wasn't afraid of Dad when Mum wasn't around. I did wonder why she was gone but knew I wasn't to ask questions. When Mum returned, there was no apparent resolution – just a return and life went on.

○

On a lovely sunny day, Mum told me to get into the car to go
to the store with her. (This is decades before seatbelts). I was
in the backseat behind Mum leaning on the back of her seat
as she started down the driveway. To go to the store with her
was a rare occurrence. Excitedly, I said, "holy balls." Mum
stopped the car. Her right arm rose in ripping power. It landed
a blast on my right cheek. In shock, I felt the burn of this brutal
act. The burn put a rock on my hurt and fear to keep it
submerged, afraid of what would be next.

She said, "Don't you ever say that again if a man ever
heard you…" she said no more. I was clueless as to why.

On a rare day, we sat at the dining room table dressed up
for a special family meal. I, at the age of twelve and feeling
smart, made a statement describing the process of body
elimination. My dad's foot caught the underside of my heavy
mahogany chair and flipped me backwards onto the floor. I
was stunned, horrified, and terrified. No one said a word or
moved. Everyone acted as though nothing happened. I felt as
though I was a complete outcast, struggling to get my dress
off my face, to free my legs and sit back up to choke food
down my knotted throat.

I missed Terrace Bay. I missed the woods. I missed biking to the store for a candy bar. I missed running games with friends among the trees. I missed my dad when he was gone.

Sometimes my dad would say, "Get up and earn your keep." I knew I had to behave, but his behaviour and words never hurt like Mum's stinging words, seething silence and unpredictable behaviour. I felt she hated me; she wished I'd never been born. I didn't feel that from Dad.

I silently cried at night while on my knees looking out my screened bedroom windowsill. I thought of running away but didn't have the guts. I hated myself for not having the guts.

One evening, a guest visited us who lived in Terrace Bay. I didn't know him; however, he named people I knew in his storytelling. I cried when I got to my bedroom. Mum heard me and asked why I was crying. I told her I missed Terrace Bay. I missed our home, the park and the people I knew. I didn't say anything about missing Dad. I didn't say anything about the tension. I never thought of it at that time. I didn't know how to say it; nor would I dare say it.

Within a few days, Dad and I drove to Terrace Bay. We drove hours on two-lane highways, then hours on one-lane highways. At times, we were on curvy gravel roads. I tried to stay awake. I was afraid Dad would fall asleep.

In our stay of two nights, we stayed with people Mum and Dad knew, but I didn't. I went to a movie with their daughter, instead of activities I'd known. My peers in school in Terrace Bay were changed to be more like my school peers in Wisconsin. They were more interested in each other as boys and girls. I was the one lagging behind in evolving. The one-year difference between our ages of eleven and twelve was evident. My heart felt misplaced.

○

Ninth grade meant high school with about 300 pupils in our class. On the first day of school, I looked up as I entered the open staircase to the second floor. The hands and faces of boys draped the ledge above me. "She looks like she belongs in kindergarten," they said, laughing. I smiled, not knowing how to take it, and kept on.

In a different first floor hallway, boys sat in chairs facing the hallway looking through the glass separation. The classroom door was open to incoming students. From the room, I heard "Moose herder" and "Bucky beaver". Again, I smiled, looking straight ahead. It wasn't lovely commenting on my protruding teeth, and the implication of their vision of where I was born, but it was attention. (My parents took me to an orthodontist that year.)

Each day, I walked to school with two girls from my high school. They lived next door to each other on the next street. They invited me to walk with them. Our walking conversations were about classes, lunch hour, the auditorium lunch hour, and their next dates with their boyfriends. I listened. The two girls had differing views they freely shared. From that, I decided I wouldn't dye my hair. I wouldn't smoke or drink. I wouldn't have sex until marriage. I thought sex was special, happening upon marriage; with only one person. These were silent commitments to myself.

On Saturday, Sandy and I walked to the public library to get books for school work. We stopped at Woolworth's Drug Store on Main Street on the way home. We sat on red stools at the grey topped counter watching our waitress make ice cream sodas. We ordered a plate of hot French fries we shared, with ketchup, and cold glasses of Coke. It was our relished treat. The look of the apple dumpling on display in the circular clear cabinet was a treat I aspired to, not yet accessible with my allowance.

○

When I turned sixteen, I worked at the Neenah Theatre. I greeted patrons through the opening in the glass window. I took cash from the lower opening, made the change (no calculator), and rang up tickets. While I worked, I heard sounds from the movie. I smelled tempting popcorn.

As people of all ages exited Alfred Hitchcock's movie, *Psycho*, they spoke of fright yet were thrilled. I heard the threatening music and screams. While working, I wanted to run from the ticket office to get a quick glimpse of the screen. In trepidation and fear, I wanted to run from the theatre, from the sounds. It was too real.

In high school, there were boys I liked and wished to date. At this time, girls didn't call or ask boys out. I loved to dance. As often as I could have permission, I attended the weekly Rec Centre evening dance where I could show up. It was informal. I danced with other girls and hoped for a special boy to ask me. During high school, there was one boy who wanted to date me many times. I felt bad that I didn't like him as a date. He was all right to talk to, but not to keep dating. In his testy humour, he said, "You have a mouth like a rose, or like a toilet plunger." (A few years after high school, a young man who was this boy's friend asked me to accompany him to a hospital. The boy I didn't savour was flat in bed. A post-surgical wound was evident. After years of him suffering headaches, and some misbehaviour, they operated (no CT scans) to find a brain tumour. My rose-shaped mouth kissed him on his cheek.

Before I had permission to go on a date, Mum asked in a non-trusting discouraging tone, who it was, who he hung around with, where he lived and how we would get there and back. I couldn't say to my caller, "Just wait a minute while I check." Her tone and the process felt arduous and heavy. It took away joy.

On my junior year prom, I wore a rare store-bought white dress with brocade flowers and high heels. I knew the boy from my classes and liked him. It was uncomfortable for both of us trying to make conversation. I liked the few dances we danced; both fast and slow.

On my senior prom, I went with a boy I didn't know well but knew who he hung around with and was excited he asked me. He hung around with people better known in our class. He was known for his sense of humour. Mum made my dress of white and periwinkle blue cotton fabric. I loved it and felt pretty with the wrist corsage he gave me. Mum said I could go to the dance, but not go to Waupaca the next day. When I accepted the prom invitation, I didn't know the tradition was to go swimming, canoeing and picnicking in Waupaca the next day. My date learned after I accepted his invitation that I couldn't go. Waupaca was forty miles away. I was devastated and embarrassed. I hated Mum, though she said she was protecting me.

When I returned from an evening date, the porch light was on. That was all right. What wasn't all right was Mum was on the other side of the door. How do we share a hug or kiss in a boundary-less moment? Quickly. When I came in, again I was questioned.

○

Before I went to high school, I knew I wanted to be a nurse. The options I knew for a career were being a teacher, a secretary or a nurse. Dad wanted me to work with computers. He was thinking of my future, however; we had no life experience with computers and I liked working with people.

My high school class choices were made with the idea of nursing school; thus, I took the required Latin, Biology, Chemistry, Algebra and Geometry. I knew I wouldn't do well in a university setting with huge classes, many students on campus, sororities and fraternities. I had to swear to become an American Citizen with Immigration in order to apply for college in the United States. I chose to apply and was accepted at St Barnabas Hospital School of Nursing, in Minneapolis, Minnesota.

We took our first-year classes of Anatomy and Physiology, Chemistry, Microbiology, and English at Macalester College in St Paul, Minnesota.

We were capped, meaning we received and wore our white nurse's cap thereafter, at the end of our first year. Our Capping ceremony was held at St Mark's Episcopal Cathedral. It was an honour. It was exciting to be on our way to being a nurse. Being capped meant we could start experiential education in the hospital along with our studies in each speciality, such as Medical-Surgical Nursing and Paediatrics.

A week after I started college in Minnesota my family moved from Neenah, Wisconsin, to Toronto, Ontario, Canada. I couldn't see my family except during Christmas break.

Instead, I went home many weekends with my roommates. It was comforting and enlightening for me because I was with a family. I participated in the family life of meals, recreation and church. It helped me see how other mums and dads interacted, and how my peers were treated at home.

We female students lived in a dorm. It was the old hospital. Our rooms were generous with bedrooms, a bathroom and a study area between bedrooms. No men were allowed in nursing in our school until my second year. No married students were allowed in the nursing program until my third year. At this time in history, men were trying to get into nursing just like more women were trying to get into medical school.

We had good food, though, a predictable menu for years, provided in the hospital cafeteria. We had a housemother, for better or worse, depending on how late you wanted to stay out. We students often said it was like living in a nunnery. We had a ten o'clock curfew on weeknights; twelve o'clock on weekends, and one o'clock once a month. We had to sign out and in. For students who dated steadily, it was confining. We had two telephones on each floor of the dorm. Those two phones were for forty students.

I had three roommates my first year, and four the second and third years. I shared a bedroom with the same roommate all three years. She was an only child. I spent many weekends with her family. My roommate sometimes sat on her dorm bed and told one joke after the other. I sat laughing on my bed. This was a great outlet at test time. Her family was part of my strength and belonging. I fondly called my roommate's parents, Uncle Bob and Aunt Ruth. Ruth was kind and Bob was funny though he looked fierce when I first met him. He said in a low voice, "What are you doing in MY chair?" I leapt out of that chair to his laughter. Both Uncle Bob and Aunt Ruth were involved in the Presbyterian Church. I loved all the hymns. I memorised a few. I softly sing or hum a hymn when I hold my grandson to help him fall asleep.

○

On the first day of our college English class, the professor said, "Write a short story." I froze. I felt the familiar, unwelcome knot of disgust for myself and terror. My pen and paper were empty. Nothing came to mind. My heart and mind couldn't start. Before the class ended, I forced myself to write something. I barely passed English.

Our anatomy lab at the Macalester College campus was disgusting, though fascinating. Our dark-haired female instructor with long fingernails fiercely pulled the mammary gland from the cat cadaver and slapped it on the metal counter creating splashes of tissue imbued with formaldehyde as she lectured. After the lab, shaking our heads at the brutal experience, we headed to the Main for lunch. We washed our hands well in the lab and applied the provided Nivea Cream. Each bite of my sandwich brought the mixed scent and unwanted vision. In our nursing labs in the dorm classrooms, we learned how to make a hospital bed, bathe, dress, and walk a patient from our Nursing Instructor, Miss Lundell. She was kind, encouraging, and displayed the attitude we would all become nurses. We learned how to give injections by practising on oranges, then on our roommates. At the end of our second year, we had to get at least a B grade on our year-long Medical-Surgical Nursing course or we were out of the nursing program. It was painful to wait for the posted grades on the dorm office wall. A few students didn't pass.

To celebrate passing, twelve of us had dinner reservations for the Waikiki Room in a Minneapolis downtown hotel. Someone had brought a bottle of liquor; dry gin from home. I'd tasted Crème de Mint and a Hot Rum Toddy, served by Dad at holiday time, but that was it. I wondered what it was like to be drunk. We shut our dorm door and got out glasses and bottles of cold 7UP. My first drink was mixed by another and handed to me. It tasted like perfume. It was wretched but I drank it, and another, and I think, another. I also smoked a cigarette, flicking ashes on the former hospital surgical suite floor. We sang and talked and I became oblivious. The next thing I knew my roommates were getting me dressed for dinner. I didn't care about dinner. I lay sideways on my back on the bed with my legs dangling as they pulled my nylons up and then coaxed me to sit up to put on my slip and blue dress. I felt sick. Into the bathroom, I went and some of what went down came up. I felt limp. Before we reached the first floor to leave the dorm, we passed a senior nursing student I knew from Neenah. I said to her, "We had so much to drink; you'd fall on your ass." I was able to walk past our housemother and get into the cab with my roommates. I was told to roll down the window and take breaths of the winter's air. Later, I was told those breaths were far deeper than wanted by them and the cab driver.

When we got to the hotel, I felt better but my roommate was sick. So off she went to the bathroom. Somehow, we managed to have dinner and pose for a group picture which says it all with a few drooping eyes and heads among smiles.

In 1963, I walked from our St Barnabas student dorm on 10th St, to Minneapolis City Hall to attend court for our nursing school Sociology Class. The court was being held for the murder trial of T. Eugene Thompson, accused of killing his wife. We waited in line in the hallway for just minutes, then were instructed to sit in the courtroom to get the full experience. Courtroom's words indicated Mrs Thompson survived the vicious attack enough to get out of the house and say words that led to finding her hired killer.

When we exited the court and walked out of the stone building onto the grey sidewalk, everyone stopped. It was announced that President John F. Kennedy was shot. Unimaginable thoughts and visions of the White House family came to mind along with fear and disbelief. Were we safe? What will happen?

○

In 1968, I was a registered nurse working in Minneapolis. I was in a men's four-bed ward along with another nurse and our janitor. From the black and white floor model TV, it was announced that Martin Luther King had been shot. The Caucasian (about 50 years old) janitor vehemently said, "They otta shoot all of 'em."

My head turned in horror and I gasped, saying, "Otto, you can't say that. That is cruel. That is wrong," Otto mumbled. I knew this man would not change his putrid attitude that horrified me. The one black patient in the room and the Native nurse said nothing. I wondered what they felt and thought.

In 1971, I applied for United States Citizenship in Minneapolis. I was pregnant with our firstborn. It was time to become a citizen. I couldn't have dual citizenship; however, I thought Canada and the United States would not go to war with each other. I took the test. My husband's aunt vouched for my integrity and I was sworn in with many ages and colours of people in the Minneapolis Courthouse. I felt honoured and welcomed the responsibility and privilege of voting.

I cast my first vote for President Nixon and Vice President Agnew. They eventually made headlines with Nixon's impeachment. During the impeachment months, I was at home with our newborn son, more than at work. I watched the trials. The trials were on TV for everyone to see and hear testimony, witnesses and evidence. It was appalling to hear what had been done and how it was covered up. In retrospect, it was far more reassuring than our first term impeachment process of President Donald Trump where there was power to prevent testimony and evidence.

○

While attending St Mark's, in my late thirties and early forties, the Director of Adult Education provided a series of classes for women to learn the history of women in America, Herstory. It was the first history class I enjoyed. It wasn't a dry lecture about dates and events; she brought history alive. We also read the book, *A History of Women in America* by Carol Hymowitz and Michaele Weissman. (Weissman)

Our teacher started the classes with how people functioned as hunters and gatherers. She brought us through the ages into the history of our own church as well as the United States. She accompanied history with real-life stories such as letters from the church archives and letters from women in history, such as Abigail Adams. Abigail Adams wrote her congressman husband, John Adams, asking him to speak up for the right to vote for women. He refused. Really. Abigail ran their home alone and cared for their children. She managed the farm, educating their children, and even dealing with rebel troops in her home during the revolution in 1775.

In class, we were invited to share our own lives and how these women in history affected us. At the end of the series, we participants decided to take one square of fabric each and create a scene or word of what woman we wanted to represent us. I chose Elizabeth Cady Stanton. I related to her being a dedicated, independent thinking mother, and her insistence that women could do far more than housework and child-rearing. She said all children should be able to wear play clothes and play outside even girls, who at that time were expected to be inside learning handwork, and housekeeping. Stanton was committed to the equality of women and stressed women needed to use their brains. From her father, who was a lawyer, she learned women had no right to divorce. She became distressed by this, as a girl, when she heard a woman tell her father what was going on, and learned the woman had no rights.

Our squares were sewn together into a colourful quilt we presented to our thrilled teacher. Her classes awakened my sense of oppression in our world, our city, our church, and my life. We heard incredible histories of the survival of women in my own church.

In January, the most frigid time of winter in Minnesota, we had experiential learning for all ages at church school called the Wayback Machine. A small room was converted into the Wayback Machine by installing a floor-model television set (TV), surrounded by cardboard walls at the front of the room. Forward-facing rows of chairs created the sense we were in a rocket ship. We entered the ship from the rear with a ticket. A video told us to get ready. We heard and excitedly joined in the loud countdown. We witnessed our take-off on the TV screen. Once the ship entered the correct time period, we heard the story.

We heard about Harriet Tubman, about St Francis of Assisi, about Abraham on the desert, and about the first ordination of women in the Episcopal Church. Participants exited through a doorway front and left to an auditorium where lighting, sounds, and life-like props created the story. For manna and quail on the desert with Abraham, empty boxes of Kentucky Fried Chicken appeared. To create escape routes for the Harriet Tubman story, flexible foil ducts crossed the floor. Young people scrambled through the ducts while hearing the sounds of dogs barking.

Five of us women wrote and re-created the scene of the first Women's Rights Convention in Seneca Falls, New York, in 1848 for the Wayback Machine. The 1848 convention was organised by Elizabeth Cady Stanton and four co-planners. Together, these women were committed to equal rights for women. Together, they wrote and spoke their words of the Declaration of Rights and Sentiments. The declaration included holding the church accountable for the oppression of women with the use of scripture. (Stanton wrote, a *Women's Bible.* Stanton couldn't get enough people to consent and acknowledge her bible. My daughter gave me a copy.)

Because Stanton had children, she did more writing rather than speaking. She and Susan B. Anthony became friends. Anthony never married and grew up in a Quaker family where equality was a given value. Susan B. Anthony spoke, often using the words written by Elizabeth Cady Stanton.

In our Wayback presentation, we included Sojourner Truth who spoke during a women's rights convention in Ohio. Sojourner had listened to clergy quoting the Bible saying women were weak and were to be subservient. A minister at the Ohio convention said women weren't strong enough to have equal rights to vote. Sojourner Truth was a thin black woman, over six feet tall. This incredible, unforgettable woman escaped from slavery in her late twenties. She became an itinerant preacher. There aren't a lot of facts known about

Sojourner. In 1997, I bought the book, *Sojourner Truth, A Life, A Symbol* by Nell Irvin Painter. Inside the cover, I wrote, "Sojourner, did you have even an inkling of how you would touch a life after many years that your physical being is gone? You touched me ten years ago and now I want to absorb you more. Thank You, God, for the gift of her being, and 'Ain't I a woman!'"

Our Wayback volunteer Sojourner was a black woman just over five feet tall but spoke the same power-filled words that exemplified unimaginable strength. Again, and again, Sojourner's refrain as a former slave who'd laboured years in cotton fields, having many of her eleven children taken from her, said, "And ain't I a woman!" (Weissman)pg101

Both Elizabeth Cady Stanton and Sojourner Truth became my wisdom figures. I thought, and think of them in times of struggle and times of celebration.

I loved our church services of majestic processions, soul-moving organ and choir music, the sacraments, especially the Eucharist at the altar.

We church school teachers bonded with our realities and dreams. Five of us camped in a state forest in Minnesota for a weekend. We called ourselves a disorder, the women of the desserts, rather than an Order, the Fathers of the Desert. We had a marvellous time tubing on a river, feasting together, and singing around our campfire.

○

Divorce. Divorce after twenty-two years. Every divorce is different just as every birth and every death is different.

My spiritual journey toward divorce involved painful labour for years, continually striving and hoping to keep our marriage alive. I loved my husband when we married. I gave myself, totally. There was no one else.

Our marriage relationship was in the dying process long before the divorce word was said, long before the legal divorce.

Divorce is a death. The process of the dying can't be discussed like one would a partner's disabling disease and pending death. It is mostly held in private. The privacy is because the relationship is sacred. Baring of the soul is sacred. Family decisions are sacred. A sexual relationship is sacred. Privacy is to protect the family as much as possible for future health. Privacy is out of respect for the other and for the marriage as it was. The marriage was not a joke.

I took my marriage vows seriously. After many years together, I felt I'd lived in indifference for at least a decade; a familiar land. It was killing me. I had learned to speak up, to ask for what I wanted to do, or wanted us to do as a couple. I learned I was allowing hurtful behaviour if I felt resentful.

We went to counselling in year seven at my request. It helped to talk in a neutral place. I learned I didn't respect myself. I went alone seven years later. The counsellor told me I had to bring my spouse next time, which I had already tried to do. It didn't make any difference after a few sessions. There was no interest from my spouse to do things together, to have a date night, or to acknowledge spiritual needs. There was no interest in who I was or how I functioned. It was a dry land, a desert.

I worked hard making a home and rearing our children. About six years prior to the legal divorce, feeling unseen, unheard, and unappreciated, I remember standing at the kitchen sink washing dishes. I thought, *I won't live this way anymore*. I had worked at adding to our marriage. Did I work too hard?

I decided to make a life for myself by letting go of my marriage expectations. Relationships with my children were paramount. In parenting, I knew ultimately my children weren't mine; they belonged to God. They had their own lives, their own opinions. None of them were adults yet, though. My outside involvements with classes, spiritual direction, meeting with an affirming women's group, and meeting with a woman friend to walk, to canoe, to see a movie became my life in addition to my children.

Again, I was continually evolving. Becoming more authentic. I didn't need constant attention from my spouse, but I needed a trickle of attention. I walked miles and miles, day after day, for years. I knew the Ten Commandments and that divorce is not acceptable. I felt I was in a bottle. I felt I was akin to a handmade wood carved ship in a bottle. I struggled to live. I pushed the cap off the bottle, breathed, and lived. Then I realised the cap was again back on the bottle. There was no life-giving air. I was dying over and over, again and again. "Until death us do part." It WAS death. I saw three cardinals in one tree. It was the sign. It was the Trinity. I told my spiritual director it was the end, the end of my marriage. She said, "The end as it is." *No, it is the end.*

My church doesn't condone divorce; however, the rector of my church said I'd be supported through it. The church was important to me for friends, the rituals, the liturgy and the words. God certainly was important to me and I married with the thought and vow, that marriage is forever. I loved God. I trusted God. There were two scriptures I'd been exposed to through spiritual direction. The first was RSV Bible, Psalm 139. The Psalm talks about how God knows us at all times and in all ways. God knows us before we know ourselves. The other was Romans 8:18–28. It talks about our suffering and how, with God's help we can become a new creation, and find freedom within the faith. It talks about how the Spirit works for us for God's purpose, and that we are never separated from God.

Psalm 139 helped me to look at myself as God would. God was a compassionate God. God saw me as I truly was, and held me in it. I cried and sat with God. God's love gave me strength, knowing no one else could begin to know what went on in my life, nor understand the reasons for what was happening. God's compassionate acceptance helped me heal; to receive the genuine love I needed to heal and change into a healthier loved and loving person. (America)

God saw me twenty-four hours a day, and knew what I was feeling, thinking, and doing. Romans 8:18 was a view of my pain. I prayed with this scripture for years. It gave me

124

comfort and hope. Previously, I'd felt I had to let go of all my dreams and be accountable to God. I trusted and felt love from God, however, I still thought I had to let go of those dreams. My relationship with God and how I saw God kept transforming. I too changed as I got to know God more and myself more. Parts of me fully died and other parts of me were dying. I began to see myself in terms of thinking about deep longings and dreams.

Having been a nurse and a mother, I witnessed and experienced birth. As scripture from Romans 8 said, "My present suffering also held glory to be revealed." I knew the glory of a newborn; God's gift. I also knew the groaning woman, me, who was to be. A new identity was birthing, and my BEING, me, the human, was working in hopeful agony, trusting. (America)

The groaning of divorce was sometimes silent, sometimes screaming. It involved not only my body and life, but the whole body of my family; spouse, children, in-laws, and friends. Divorce does affect generations, though there is healing, too, for healthier lives. God listens to our sighs, the silent utterances, not noted even by me. God heard them.

There was comfort in the agony because of my trust in God. I continued to make a life for myself with the painting classes. I began to drop expectations. I was a planner. I realised childhood experiences had subconsciously taught me to constantly watch, to listen, to try to feel what others felt around me so I could prepare for what might come; to avoid condemnation. I had to become more flexible, and more spontaneous. I began to have fun with my woman friends, even with a couple who asked us to go for a boat ride. My husband said no. I went without him.

One day, the divorce word was said aloud. The word fell out of my mouth. My husband took me out to dinner in a fine restaurant. He never did that. No matter how much I intellectually still wanted to stay together, emotionally, I couldn't do it anymore. Out came the deadly divorce word. I didn't want this for my family. I was angry with God. I'd prayed and prayed for a healthy marriage step by step for miles.

My husband and I decided we'd stay together until we worked out our divorce agreement without lawyers. It was okay and it was hard. The court referee congratulated us on our plan. The plan didn't follow the normal guidelines of child support. It was financially creative so I could keep our home and my ex-husband would be able to have his own place. I didn't ask for alimony. Part of my decision about alimony was I wanted the children and their dad to do it all right. I also thought, *I'll take care of myself. I'll do without your damn money*. Monthly, we shared the list of expenses for the children; however, expenses reveal values – differing values. We didn't always agree on what was essential. It became harder and harder, more stressful. The day he didn't include money for a bouquet of flowers for my daughter's music teacher after my daughter's piano recital, I was furious. I'd had it.

It wasn't worth an exhausting confrontation over ten dollars. It wasn't the first time I'd let go, not only about money; but child care issues, like supporting counselling for a child after the first twelve sessions were completed that insurance allowed. As in the Bible scripture 1 Kings 3:26, I didn't want to cut the baby in half by forcing a decision.

I went downstairs to the storage closet. I found the zippered protective clothing bag. I unzipped and removed my saved, precious, beautiful wedding gown. I laid it on the floor and got on my knees. I gripped my silver-handled sharp sewing scissors. In an abject rage, screaming and yelling, *the end* tears flew.

I cut and cut and cut it up.

○

Less than a year after our legal divorce I took my children to a family church camp in northern Minnesota. I had no idea how vulnerable I was. Though I still cried, I thought I was strong. I'd get upset with myself, shaking my head in disbelief when I saw a couple together, thought they had a perfect life, and yearned for what I thought they had.

While at camp, a man working at the camp paid attention to me during campfires. He paid attention to my youngest daughter. He asked if he could visit and take me out. He spoke of religion in his life. He knew camp songs about God and Jesus. I thought God was giving me a gift. I was wrong. I didn't listen to my inner nudges when he was vague about his past life, and his current full-time work. We swiftly married in a chapel at church with a reception of friends in my, now, our home.

I knew the first year, I'd made a huge mistake. I was ashamed and exhausted. It took me six years to file for divorce. My husband lied, was unpredictable and disappeared for days. He hurt us, he hurt his work, and he hurt his past family. He was a parasite. He harassed us, my youngest daughter and me, with phone calls at home and at my work, even to my boss.

I had to get a lawyer, pay a lawyer. At first, the lawyer didn't think I was being sympathetic with my disturbed husband. The lawyer learned when we had to get the divorce decree to my evading husband via a sheriff.

My desire to share about faith and religion, my desire to belong, to be touched, and sex led me to see what I wanted to see.

I got a restraining order AFTER divorce, without a lawyer. The bailiff at the courtroom door gave me a card for Harriet Tubman Shelter as I left. He said I could call them if I needed any more help. God, what a mess. *Please forgive me. Children, please forgive me.*

How can I trust myself?

○

Let me tell you one-way new life began.

Early in my career with new-borns, I worked with a well-seasoned, faith-filled nurse who was an advocate of breastfeeding. I was privy to her being with new mothers and babies; the opening of the blanket to fully embrace their newborn and learn how to put mother and baby together for mutual nourishment. The nurse exuded confidence and joy for both baby and mother.

RSV Bible Psalm 131:2 was evident:

'But I have calmed and quieted my soul,
like a weaned child with its mother;
my soul is like the weaned child that is with me.'
(America)

I remembered the nurse as I sketched a vision inspired by the scripture. I thought that must be how God Mother is. My relationship with God, my divine mother, woman, and the feminine grew.

My anger about being a woman, thought to be less, not as mentally and emotionally strong as a man with less opportunities, was beginning to transform. I had anger about

130

my past and the imposed silence of my whole being – the destruction by my mum – another woman. My inner being was now disturbed by destructive actions against women and people of colour, about labels in education, about the injustice of women's situations all over the world, and in my own little world.

I realised in my vulnerability, and in my humanity, that I'd given all my power to God, suspending all judgement – not just suspending being judgmental. In thinking of the ensuing people and events in my life that hurt me and others; I began to realise women are not weak. I began to realise I needed to make wise judgements; different from being judgmental.

I became grateful I was a woman. I had a deeper sense of courage and strength as a mother. Our world and society do harm by promoting one gender or personality as better, rather than different. I saw again and again how out of my womanhood and willingness to be vulnerable; I had made wise decisions. I had courage and strength, and I needed to make judgements.

At about age fifty, I wrote these words in my journal.

Divine Mother

Given to me in quiet,
you appeared and have transformed as I transform.
You, a distinct being, so perfect for me.
I wouldn't know what to ask for.
The One who knew and gave me what I needed and far more.

You come to me at the water's edge;
you sit on a rock and wait and watch me.

You come into the water with me and I immerse
even more into your cleansing love.
You hold me in the water as though I was a young babe.
We play in the water as free souls.
You know what's in my heart;
I need not say a word.
You listen with the ears of the whole universe;
you listen to one little soul.
You are never rushed.
How marvellously you listen to the unspoken.
How wonderfully you let me know we are women.
You do this by just being;
you don't have to announce it.
It is just there to celebrate.
You are steadfast and honest.
I never have to wonder if you are straight with me.
Oh, how wondrous that is to trust and know
you and you fully.
You aren't impressed by material goods or power.
You do not hide.
You are not timid.
You love all.
You reverence all.
You are distressed by discounting of anyone.
You know we all have something to contribute.
You know we are vulnerable and able to be touched.
It is a gift to be open to touch.
It is the gift of love to you and the universe.
In turn, it is what opens us to you.
My heavenly Mother,
how grateful I am for you.

We enjoy each other,
and you are always there for me.
I hope I am there for you. (Cogger)

○

Now living alone in my home, I was grateful I survived. I was beginning to thrive. My last child was in college. I had work. I was healthy.

For fun and for my health, I joined a walk for breast cancer, honouring a family member, and a walk for ALS (Amyotrophic Lateral Sclerosis), honouring a friend.

I had a new desire – to run – after an unplanned witnessing of a marathon. The Twin Cities of Minneapolis and St Paul, Minnesota, hold a Twin Cities Marathon in the fall.

I started parking my car two blocks from work and running. I tried running around the lake I had walked for years but found I couldn't run. One day, I slowed down and realised I could run at a slower pace, more like a walking jog. I got *a Running Magazine.* I was inspired by the short stories. From there, I prepared for a walk/run around Lake Nokomis. I motivated myself by telling myself I was getting healthier by outrunning my fears. It worked.

I hadn't witnessed the Twin City Marathon; however, I decided to enter the 5K run. It was held the day before the marathon in 1995.

I stood in the middle of seasoned runners and families who would walk. The gun went off. I started my slow, steady run. I felt and heard the whoosh of the seasoned crowd run by me, their force pulling me. The force dropped. I wondered if I was the only one left. I decided not to look back. I kept going up the hill, then up even more on the long Wabasha Bridge over the river in downtown St Paul. As I was going up the bridge, runners were already racing back down the bridge. Some people who were walking decided to turn back. I kept going. I made it up and down the bridge and back to Harriet Island where we started. As I approached the last fifty feet, a voice enthusiastically yelled, "Go Dawn!" What a lift. It gave me a speed boost and was a welcome sound, made by a co-worker whose father was running. I had no idea anyone was there who knew me. I made it, going through the same gates the marathoners would go through the next day. What a thrill. I had my picture taken with my hands gleefully in the air, shouting joy, number 1251 on my jacket.

O

My office in my position at a 300-bed long-term skilled care facility was on the third floor at the beginning of the fifty resident nursing station. (People in a hospital are addressed as patients. People in an LTC facility are called residents) Our LTC facility administrator asked me to bring my dog, Spritz to work. He met Spritz when my daughter had visited the facility, bringing Spritz with her. Family visitors brought in pets. Most residents loved it. Bringing Spritz to fit in with my job of keeping up the spirits of staff, as well as residents; a request from my boss, our CEO.

Spritz, our blond cocker spaniel with a curl on top, loved work too. I tried to bring her weekly depending on my workload. In the morning she'd sit attentively, eyes fixed on me, as I dressed for work. She seemed to understand the weekly cycle. On her visiting day, I'd look at Spritz and say, "Do you want to go to work?" She leapt two feet in the air. She ran to the doorway. She pulled her leash off the hook. She wagged her short tail across the floor, sitting and waiting for me with the handle of her leash in her mouth. The tail wag propelled a body wag. With the handle of her leash still in her mouth, she pranced beside me to the car.

I hung onto the leash once in the facility. Otherwise, she took off, her blond cocker ears flying in the air like Dumbo the elephant. Depending on the summoning scent she ran to the dining room if it was mealtime or the happy hour lounge with spilt popcorn. She ignored my commands. I told Spritz we'd both be fired for such behaviour. Her quick unexpected escape brought waves of residents' laughter as I caught her. A resident said, "Ah, leave her. She can sleep on my bed anytime."

A resident who lived on the third floor often came by my door. We'd say hello and wave to each other. The resident was slowly losing physical abilities and memory. She was aware of her debilitating disease until she wasn't.

She walked into my office. It wasn't common for her to enter. She frowned and tried to explain. The words wouldn't come. She couldn't move her arms or hands to express herself. Her deepening frown said she was frustrated, becoming more disturbed. I stood. I slowly approached her. I asked her if she needed something. She uttered confusing words about her family, thinking they hadn't come. She couldn't remember their last visit. I asked her if I could give her a hug. She nodded yes, with pleading eyes. I put my arms beneath her limp arms wrapping them around her. I brought her to my chest. Her chest heaved. As I held her, sobs and a runny nose came. I wiped her nose. "What a friend," came out clearly. I asked her if she'd like to sit. Spritz was tethered to my desk leg. Spritz stood and watched attentively. With my help, the resident sat in my green armless office chair. I got on my knees on the beige carpet beside her. I asked her if she'd like me to pray with her, for her. I knew her religious choice and knew she prayed. She'd previously shared with me she was going to tell God a lot when she got to heaven. As we put our hands together on her knees, Spritz, put her head there too. I prayed a simple prayer for the resident's health, her safety and wellbeing, and her family, all into God's abiding. With my head still lowered and eyes closed, I waited for words she might add. I slowly raised my head to see her smiling face looking at Spritz. She said, "Two great women and a dog." We laughed.

○

My bedside phone rang at four in the morning. Answering it, I quickly awakened when my LTC administrator said he needed me to come to work immediately. He explained the water main in the four-lane street in front of our complex had exploded, creating a large hole in the street. As a result, we had lost water for our 300 bed skilled nursing facility and our attached 300 independent living apartments. On any given day there were 300 to 400 staff working too. He said the Director of Nursing and Assistant Director of Nursing were out of town at a conference for two more days. My job as Director of Staff Development and Infection Control included general orientation of all staff as well as the ongoing education of nursing staff, and infection control in both buildings.

Our Director of Purchasing had already ordered thirty port-a-potties for staff, resident, and tenant use. He'd purchased gallon-sized plastic bottles of water for drinking water and minimal bathing. He purchased hundreds of individual bottles of hand sanitiser for all residents, staff and tenants. He had already distributed the water and sanitisers. Under normal conditions, nursing staff washed their hands with soap and warm running water, rubbing hands, fingers and thumbs briskly for at least twenty seconds. Then rinse, then dry using a paper towel, turn off the water with the paper towel and throw it in the receptacle near the open door. The technique is done before, after, and during resident, and tenant care as well as after staff personal use of the bathroom and before eating. If preferred, and certainly at this time with a water problem, staff were allowed to use alcohol-based gel hand sanitisers.

Normally when city water mains are flushed and we temporarily lose water pressure at home, it creates inconvenience. And, we're given a warning so we can have water available for drinking and cooking. We avoid doing laundry and avoid flushing toilets for that brief time.

In a healthcare setting where many people are in one area with different germs, proper hand washing and the disposal of body waste are vital to infection control. Physical care, like bathing and nutrition, are necessary too. The loss of water created major challenges that required a shift in priorities and procedures.

By 6 am, all department heads were in a meeting with our administrator. Challenges were brought forward. The kitchen juice dispensers didn't work because they run by water pressure. The walk-in freezer was run by circulating water and would start to thaw. Because of the number of people to feed, disposable dishes and cutlery had to be used. Nursing staff had to be advised to watch residents who might break off a piece of plastic in their mouth and choke. The meals were kept simple in terms of cooking and clean-up. There was fresh food. When our purchasing person stopped at a local fast-food restaurant to buy his breakfast when getting bottled water. He explained the situation. The restaurant offered to make hot coffee if we brought our containers for transport. That was a gift. Our department heads refreshed our memories of where the wall fire extinguishers were. The automatic sprinklers wouldn't work without water. Because we didn't fit the Red Cross definition of disaster, they couldn't help us. The fire department couldn't help us. The Department of Transportation said it would take hours to find and repair the water main problem.

One of the pluses of my job was that I knew every employee in the complex. Everyone hired came to me for fifteen-minute health history and received a Mantoux (a skin test to see if they've been exposed to the infectious disease, Tuberculosis). In that brief time, moments were shared about our lives.

Trying to lighten the forthcoming work burden, I asked residents and staff to pretend we were camping. We would use hand sanitiser for hands, use portable toilets, if possible, and do minimal bathing. Food would be served in the usual places on disposable dishes. I continually made rounds on the six nursing stations, helping as needed, checking supplies, listening to concerns, and assisting with care assessment. I learned many residents were afraid or not willing to use portable toilets. Also, some staff had never used one and were afraid too. I could understand the huge challenge of taking a resident from their room and nursing station, down on the elevator, and outside to the portable toilets. Too much. We had a few commodes. Mostly, though, toilets had to be used. No flushing. We got through two meals and morning cares with minimal problems.

At 2 pm, our administrator informed us he'd notified the Minnesota Department of Health (MDH) of our situation. They didn't have any alternatives to offer. Our normal policies were to use the water main if we had an emergency for water. Obviously, we needed to change the future policy to add more than one alternative. MDH was at least aware of our challenge in case there were complaints. Supper was planned. Soiled linens were piled to the laundry ceiling. Some linens had been taken to a laundry and brought back. It might need to be done again.

The Director of Maintenance and Director of Purchasing, God bless them, remembered we had an old well on the property used years before to water lawns. Those two men and our administrator decided to explore the option. Digging in the dirt was tangible hope. By 4 pm the men hooked up several consecutive garden hoses. They brought the hose into the facility by removing the upper part of a first-floor utility room window. The hose draped across a hallway floor where three large empty laundry carts were filled with water. The carts were over four feet high. Only two people could fit in the elevator with one cart. I checked infection control policies for emergency disinfection of water. We would not use the water for anything except the toilets but still added bleach for disinfecting. The Director of Maintenance and I worked together on one floor which included two stations – 100 residents. He dipped and lifted the full pail of water from the cart. I carried the full pail into the resident bathroom. I looked at the toilet that hadn't been flushed since 4 am, over twelve hours ago with two to four people using the bathroom. The toilet was full to the bottom of the rim with multicoloured solid and liquid body waste and used toilet paper. I hoped and prayed the pail of water would work, knowing I had to pour fast enough to get the waste to move, and slow enough so I wouldn't make a bigger mess. I poured. The water swirled and took the toilet contents like magic. I've never felt such immediate job satisfaction. It was a pleasure to flush the next 69 toilets.

By supper time, energy was waning, especially among tired residents with all sorts of maladies. At 8 pm water flowed from the repaired water main. It was determined a small gas leak from a nearby pipe triggered the explosion, which broke the water pipe. The disaster could have been much worse. Everyone had worked together. We ended up in high spirits.

○

When the Activity Director of the apartment complex said she invited an inspirational speaker for the tenants, I asked to hear more. When I heard the speaker's topic and name, I was excited, yet calmly said, "I think I know him, mind if I come?"

It was who I thought it was. I was cautious about meeting him one to one but wanted to. I was cautious out of respect. This man had been a patient of mine. He'd had a drastic change in life. I didn't know if he'd want to see me.

The first time I met him, he was just out of high school. He'd been hit by a drunk driver. The accident caused a spinal cord injury and paralysis. I was the Head Nurse of his unit. He was with us for many months.

When the young man left us to go to a more appropriate facility for his age, he didn't leave my heart. I often wondered how he was doing. To this day, I remember him when I hear songs by singer John Denver, who was beginning to shine in his own brief life.

About ten years later, I saw a catalogue of Christmas cards put out by Courage Center in Minneapolis, Minnesota. To my joy, his picture and cards were in there. His art was created by keen use of art tools using his mouth. The center had a display and he was there. I didn't speak with him but was grateful to see him and be part of his world.

This appearance at our apartment complex was another twenty or so years later. I greeted him. We spoke briefly, with smiles, and remembering. As he spoke to the group, he talked about his accident, his paralysis from the shoulders down, and his journey, which included major struggles. He told them what he could do and not do. He shared how he could be greeted since he couldn't shake hands; touch his shoulder instead. He shared how he came to become a man of faith; how it changed his life. It was awesome for me to remember him at age eighteen, and now see who he was – an inspirational speaker, a steadfast man. While listening, I thought, *you are a picture of resurrection to me.*

○

I treated myself. I made a solo car trip, to a love, Terrace Bay, Ontario, Canada. On the way, I stayed at Naniboujou Lodge, built in the 1920s with a two-story fireplace. It's on Lake Superior, north of Grand Marais, Minnesota. I brought my watercolours and a mini tape recorder. I hiked across the street from Naniboujou and found the trail I yearned to hike again. I saw pink Lady Slippers. My mind photographed them to paint later. I stood at the top of the swirling waters of the Devil's Kettle. Seeing the swirling depth of the water with an unknown outlet reminded me of my surrender to God. I hiked only a few miles of the Lake Superior Hiking Trail, reminding myself I was alone.

I drove further north. I stopped to see the vistas of Lake Superior. I saw a full rainbow across the front view of my car just before crossing the border into Ontario, Canada. Closer to Terrace Bay and Lake Superior, Rossport was still the quaint fishing village, though I didn't see any fishing boats and fishermen. I drove into Terrace Bay passing the familiar breath-taking, Aquasabon Gorge. I went to the recreation centre and again loved seeing the pictures on the walls with the history of Terrace Bay. Dad and Mum were in some of the pictures. I fondly reflected on my years growing up in Terrace Bay.

I drove behind McCausland hospital. I stood on the shore of Lake Superior. I saw where the sky met water; the joining of heaven and earth. The water from the gorge pooled, and then entered the lake. Using a cup of water from Lake Superior, I attempted watercolour painting while sitting on a bed of stones. To my left were miles of open beach with waves breaking on the shore.

My thoughts travelled to 'our boy'. A feather floated by. In wonder, my eyes and inquiring heart followed it. The feather came from nowhere. It's one of those feathers found closest to the bird's body, a piece of fine down, pure white and delicate. It landed on the still pool of water and drifted toward me. I thought, *it's our boy*, as I imagined heaven for him. He would be running on the beach in the powerful breakers coming from the deep centre, and return. The bird feather sat on the water and moved gently. It came within a foot of me. It surprised me by shifting and travelling in the opposite direction, out to the main lake. I didn't notice any shift in the wind or ripples on the water. The pure white feather sat on top of the water. It was gentle and delicate; that's what gave it strength. It travelled a great distance until I couldn't see it. I imagined it in the middle of the lake, the seaway, the ocean, and I finally let 'our boy' go, knowing we are all connected.

O

In November 2002, I remarried. I still lived in my Minnesota home, working full-time, and involved in my labours of love. When life led to remarriage.

My spouse-to-be lived in Maryland. We started communicating because my ex-spouse and he knew each other from high school in Wisconsin. After high school, they met again at our 40th high school reunion (all three of us had gone to the same high school). I chose not to go to the reunion. It was my daughter's 21st birthday. I wanted to be with her as she would soon return to college. After the two men conversed at the reunion, I received phone calls from both of them, telling me what happened. Their conversations ended with my ex-spouse giving him my phone number. He encouraged him to call me too. Both of them were excited when they each relayed their talk.

Do I want to venture here again?

I had continued meeting monthly with my counsellor. I had told her I needed a cheerleader during and after my second divorce. The cost was a stretch and worth every penny.

When I got my future husband's call asking me to get together with him, to meet him at his timeshare in Florida, I felt like a locomotive was headed my way, even though this man was usually quiet. I said we didn't really know each other though I knew of him. In high school, he was quiet, studious and didn't get in any trouble. We started with long hand letters to see if we wanted to be friends. We wrote about what we did, what we wanted to do, and asked questions. Next came the phone calls. We both had home and work computers; however, I didn't want to communicate by email. He sent me a tiny tape recorder. He sent tapes in addition to our phone calls. When the first tape arrived, I wondered how he expected me to listen to it, and then record it back on the provided tape. I had a job, a life, and children. He was single, had a home, and travelled extensively with his work.

The tapes told me how he loved early morning. How he drove to Pennsylvania to see his sister, nieces and nephews. He shared an experience of feeling saturated in God's love.

After several months, we met at my home. He had come from Maryland, driving his sister and four children, to Wisconsin to visit his widowed mother for Christmas. From there, he drove the 300-mile trip to Minneapolis. My three adult children were present due to a Christmas gathering. They were sceptical.

From there it progressed to many phone calls learning what each of us wanted. We spent many minutes talking about food as he often called at my supper time. Then the expression of love and the big question came. It was scary and exciting. I wondered if I could trust myself. I wondered if I could change my life again.

We married in my sister's Vermont home with my adult children, our siblings, his mother and my parents. My dad was dying. I wanted him there.

We wrote our own service using, *the Book of Common Prayer, Native Spirituality*, and a quote from St Hildegard of

Bingen about the energy of new beginnings. A friend of my sister's, a Justice of the Peace, presided.

My new husband took a job in North Carolina still connected with his current work. We had talked at length about where we wanted to live. I had wanted to warm up for years but hadn't been able to travel to see where I might re-establish myself. One of my long-time friends had previously told me about her beloved home state of North Carolina.

I was able to retire. It was hard to leave my adult children. I hoped they'd all join us for a holiday in our North Carolina home. We both started a new life. Everything was new.

A group of women in Minnesota gave me a three-wick large white candle I burned every day while transitioning. The group was called Wild Grace. It was a group where I/we could be the women we were, supported and encouraged to be all we were meant to be. We listened and affirmed our own truth and gifts. Their presence brought me strength and courage.

After we moved to North Carolina, my husband worked for six more years and then retired. I became involved in taking art classes, and in the Episcopal Church. Across the street from the main Episcopal Church was a small former mission church, St Phillip's.

A noonday Holy Eucharist and Healing service was held weekly. I entered the chapel where there was one parishioner and our female priest. Since there were only the three of us, we gathered at the altar.

During our time at the altar, I sensed Dad's presence coming from behind me. He gently put his arms around my waist. He placed his head so the side of his face touched the side of my face where it had burned with pain from the slap by my mum. Dad's touch was a precious balm. Then his essence moved. As he moved in front of me and seemed to be leaving, I saw his arm and hand outstretched to me while he said, in silence, "Come we're going to be fed." Meaning Eucharist to me.

Though I'd taken a few art classes in Minnesota in my forties, I hadn't had time to routinely draw and paint. Through volunteering at the art council in our new home, I met artists, learned about our area and began to make friends. I took adult education classes. I began to be freer with my approach, learn more about watercolour painting, and started painting with acrylics too. Painting classes became a priority. With another artist, our art was displayed for a Friday night Art walk. It was exciting. I shared my love for art at church too. We painted words from scripture or other inspirational statements. We then shared with each other and ended with a brief Holy Eucharist service with the priest.

Though I doubt my art will ever be famous (I've learned not to say "never"), I am an encouraging person for others to become creative. I've had the joy of painting with all my grandchildren as soon as they can paint without sucking on the paintbrush. Now that is joy. The other bonus was, as an artist peer said, "How great to be with a gaggle of artists."

◯

Shortly after participating in Bible study at the Episcopal Church, I was asked to become a Lay Eucharistic Visitor. The training involved teaching by our priest and visiting shut-ins in their home or care facilities with another Eucharistic Visitor, until comfortable on my own.

The Eucharistic Visit includes taking time to have a conversation, to let the shut-in parishioner know who I was, to ask how they were, and to listen. I started the brief service of prayers and providing communion with, "Is there anything you'd like me to pray for?" The question invited concerns and joys. The communion box contained the pre-consecrated wafers, wine and tiny plate and wine chalice. I was doing what I loved. I relished meeting new people and hearing their life memories, past and present. The challenge was to keep the visit to 20–30 minutes so I could visit the two to three people on that Sunday after church. The people I visited wanted to know where I came from, and more about me. They asked about people in the congregation they no longer saw due to their isolation. They asked about the church. They asked about the service. I shared what I could. I learned a lot from them about my new church, community and, especially how they longed for their church family.

I talked with our woman priest. I asked her what she thought about us having a monthly gathering at St Phillip's Church, bringing the shut-ins together.

Our priest gave the okay. She smiled, telling me to make sure the time didn't conflict with bridge games. Initially, I talked with family members of the to-be guests. The major challenge of transportation had to be arranged. When we advertised the monthly group, we invited anyone who wanted to participate in the group of elders, hoping active parishioners would come too. They did. About six shut-in people came and about six were active in the community. We started with a topic such as bringing a photo of a pet, or a favourite life memory. Each one shared during the hour around our table. The storytelling and discussion that followed was lively and enlightening. One person talked about gas street lamps in New York, where he had lived. One woman talked about recently driving from California where she had lived, back to North Carolina. This tiny woman drove in the heat of summer in her pickup truck with no air conditioning. She stopped at a motel, went through the lobby to the swimming pool, took a swim, got back in her truck and again drove in the cooling wet of her clothes. How we laughed in raised eyebrow astonishment.

We had lunch, provided by active church members not involved in the group. Over the four years we met, we occasionally had a menu request from residents of facilities. We tried to fulfil the request. My retired husband cooked when the request was a ham dinner. If a priest was available, we had Holy Eucharist and Healing in the chapel after lunch. If no priest, a faithful, faith-filled parishioner provided a noonday Prayer on her work lunch break.

I facilitated the group and was often transporter from facilities. My physical energy was changing. It was time to let go and start something new.

During noonday services by our priest, she gave a brief history of a person of faith in history I found fascinating. In May of 2010, the Episcopal Church published the book, *Holy Women, Holy Men: Celebrating the Saints*.[3] I asked if anyone was interested in a monthly group to learn more about the saints. A friend gave me the book. Anywhere from six to twelve of us met monthly at St Phillip's.

We took turns presenting the information we gleaned from the book and our own research. None of us who started in the group were theologians. A few of the people we studied were: Teresa of Avila, John Muir, Lydia, Phoebe, Reverend Pauli Murray, Harriet Bedell, David Pendleton Oakerhater, Meister Eckhart and Julian of Norwich. It was fun to learn and exciting to hear each person present, not only because of the saint but because the presenter shared why they chose this person. Creativity abounded with music, pictures, quotes and more. Before ending each session, we each had the opportunity to share our thoughts. At the end of each school year, we celebrated with a litany of the stories presented. Our last Litany of Remembrance was May 2015.

○

A woman who was a part of the Emmaus Christian Ecumenical Retreat Group in North Carolina told me about the retreat group. The group met on the last Monday morning of every month. The group was composed of retired clergy, laymen and women. Dr Richard Batzler and Joan Fenner, started the group thirty years ago.

I'd been in North Carolina for at least five years now and needed a group to spiritually feed me. The Emmaus group became my priority. It, too, was a group that invited others to lead and share. Upon opening the door to the Emmaus group, I was met with a welcome by Dr Batzler (now deceased). He was a learned man who had vast formal education in theology and psychology. He had varied, extensive ministry and life experiences. He wrote, painted, and had radical openness to and for everyone, always focusing on the positive, God. Joan Fenner has formal education in education, in faith and retreat formation through the Cenacle in New York State. She has life and faith experiences of many years with wide open arms to all who come. Joan, in my words, was nudged by God to share her gifts and a desire to offer retreats. She and Dr Batzler were introduced to each other and the Emmaus Ecumenical Christian Retreat Group was formed.

The Emmaus retreat presenter follows a format. Introductions of new and old participants are followed by an initial centring quiet time. From there, a group prayer brings us together with an openness to receive. The presenter gives a presentation on a topic, such as *the Wonder of God's Love*. The presentation includes why that personal choice of topic, and fifteen minutes on the topic. A hand-out is provided with a wealth of scripture, readings, and other related fodder. Forty-five minutes are allotted for individual quiet time. A participant can sit anywhere in the large room used for education, meetings and services. A table of light refreshments is sprinkled with goodies from, and for anyone in the gathering. A soft bell is rung after the forty-five minutes of quiet. Participants meet in small groups of 2–3 to share the fruit of their quiet time. After twenty minutes in small groups, everyone gathers again in the circle of chairs where anyone can share in the large group. A closing prayer and hugs of peace are shared with goodbyes for those who need to leave. Some of us stayed to share the feast with each other with our bag lunches. Those lunches become a banquet like the loaves and fishes…the literal and spiritual food multiplied.

Through our meetings and sharing deep friendships formed. I too facilitated retreats. It was a labour of love to put a retreat together. When beginning the process of gathering materials and thoughts, I'd have to restrain myself to keep from sitting for hours reading old and new materials. It was life-giving.

In 2016, my husband and I started moving back to the Midwest, to Wisconsin. He'd retired in 2006 and we had the joy of travel to see our families, and to see a lot of the world. I learned I had macular degeneration, an eye disease affecting vision. My mum, aunt and grandmother all developed the disease. Fortunately, it takes a long time to destroy central vision; however, I knew we needed to be near family. We found a residence near one of my adult children in Wisconsin. We gradually moved ourselves from our North Carolina home and gardens to a place where our snow is shovelled, and grass mowed for us.

The Emmaus group continues in my life via internet sharing of retreat materials. Joan Fenner sends retreat materials monthly. This has been especially appreciated during our COVID isolation.

○

When I still lived in Minneapolis in 1988, a group from my Christian parish went to the Holy Land. I wanted to go. I had a young family and a full-time nursing position. It was impossible. A thoughtful parishioner asked if she could carry my written prayer and place it in the Wailing Wall (now called the Western Wall). My cherished note said, "I believe, help my unbelief."

While living now, in North Carolina, I received the latest copy of *Presence,* the International Journal of Spiritual Direction. (I joined Spiritual Directors International in 1995). The Journal advertised an international ten-day Interfaith-Pilgrimage to Israel and Palestine in 2010. While reading the ad, I blurted out, "I'm so excited." *This is perfect*, I say to myself as I read more. Then, while setting the journal on the kitchen table, I dismiss the idea as non-reachable and walk away.

My husband was sitting at the kitchen table as I stood examining the offer. The next day, my husband, who had been to the Holy Land on business before we married, said, "I think you should go. You can go."

"Really, you think so?" I responded. He gave an affirmative nod. Minutes later, I proclaimed, "I'm going!"

My ongoing spiritual transformations fostered me to become increasingly inclusive of all faiths. Joyce McFarland, one of my initial supervisors at the Cenacle, who was also part of the SDI team that wrote ethics for spiritual direction, gave me these calligraphed words in 1989: '*Our first task in approaching another people, another culture, another religion is to take off our shoes for the place we are approaching is HOLY. Else we may find ourselves treading on another's dream...more serious still, we may forget that God was there before our arrival.*'

The Pilgrimage Began

Our SDI pilgrimage guides were Pastor Don Mackenzie, Rabbi Ted Falcon and Sheikh Jamal Rahman.[4] The three religious men had been working together since 9-11-2001. They lived in the Washington state area. They became friends and spiritual companions for each other. They taught, wrote and promoted inter-faith dialogue together. They became known as the Three Interfaith Amigos. All of them have a sense of humour, evident when you witness them together.

All 49 of us pilgrims from four continents (S. Africa, Ireland, Peru, North America) stayed at St George's College in Jerusalem. www.sgcjerusalem.org

My room at the college was in the guesthouse. It was a brief walk on an uneven stone walkway from the college, past the cathedral and through a stone archway. My generous bedroom was walls of grey stones with a spherical shaped ceiling. A solid-wood door entered into the hallway with daylight beaming from the lush courtyard of colourful, tempting grapefruit and orange trees.

On the first morning in Jerusalem, I was rudely awakened at 4 am by the Islamic call to worship. The call to worship is prayed over a loudspeaker. I wondered how I would approach it if I lived there and wasn't a Muslim. Thereafter, I appreciated the Islamic call to prayer more each day.

Each day, we met after breakfast for a meditation guided by one of our peers. Our group was composed of Christians, Jews and one Muslim. The meditations provided an invitation to experience out of our own sphere, both the religion and the person presenting. The morning meditation steadied us to walk in peace. We wanted to walk in inner peace wherever we went. We did not want to bring discord to any historical or holy site, or any passing person.

We were told the word Israel means persistence for God. Jerusalem means peace that comes from wholeness.

On day one we travelled by bus to the Mount of Olives. The view across the valley is the Old City of Jerusalem, including what's left of the Western Wall. It was destroyed by the Romans in 70ce. Only the foundations of the Western Wall remain today, the holiest site in Judaism. The Mount of Olives side of the hill, where we were standing, includes the oldest operating traditional Jewish cemetery. It is unbelievably vast, and parts of it have been disturbingly desecrated. My quiet sobs came. *What we do to each other again and again.* In the valley below is the Christian cemetery and the Muslim cemetery is adjacent, just below the wall of the city of Jerusalem.

At each sacred place of the three religions, the local guides told us about the historical site. At each sacred place, each of the Three Interfaith Amigos took five minutes to tell us more in terms of their religions. My intent is to share what I remember; accompanied by my own experience.

We entered the Garden of Gethsemane, where we could wander, hug an olive tree, or sit. Pastor Don said, "We, too often are not awake, and cannot be awake all the time."

From the Garden of Gethsemane, we could see the Islamic Dome of the Rock across the valley. Imam Jamal said, "The Dome of the Rock is important to Islam because Muhammad went to the mountains to meditate often; even for forty days (which means enough time). He ascended seven levels into the heavens (vertical journey) as he journeyed horizontally from Mecca to Jerusalem." Imam Jamal added, "The Quran talks about spaciousness; that my inner space gives me outer space. We have a fulfilling life when we're working in both parts of our life – the visible and the invisible. When we praise God, we become holier."

Rabbi Ted said, "Remember too that Jesus was a Jew in the Garden of Gethsemane, and other Jews (like the guards) didn't like what Jesus was doing. The Jews wanted a peacemaker."

The co-director of the pilgrimage and Executive Director of SDI, reminded us, "We are being prayed for by 7,000 SDI members."

I accidentally left my hat at Gethsemane. To me, it was symbolic of me leaving who I was. A new beginning.

Later that evening, we heard the moving presenter, Dalia Landau from the Open House Peace Centre. She is one of the characters in the non-fiction book, *the Lemon Tree*. Dalia told us about her experiences of being a girl of 19 in 1967 in Israel after the six-day war. She said, "I was in an attitude of miracles. Israel was saved. I was studying in the army. Three strange men in dress suits came to my gate (Palestinians). Do I respond or not? She thought. She went to the gate. 'This is my parents' home; can we see it?' one of the Palestinian men said." While Dalia Landau spoke, she purposefully walked back and forth in the classroom, within our circle of pilgrims. Her bright-red hair bounced. Her vibrancy of voice and body matched her bouncing hair. "What would YOU do?" she asked. Another of her statements stuck with me. "Instead of thinking of Jerusalem as the bride with more than one suitor, we need to think of her as the mother. A mother loves more than one child."

Dalia's presentation and the book have given me a perspective of the holy land I didn't have. I have compassion for all people there, their religions, their cultures and their desires to keep sacred places sacred. All these thoughts, meanings and desires are important, yet can be used to hurt each other. There is no easy solution.

In our evening classroom circle, Rabbi Ted led us in Shabbat. He said, "Prayers are our yearnings. Shabbat is accepting – a blessing for all that is and isn't."

Pastor Don said, "That moment of 'share in remembrance of me,' was institutionalised into a sacrament from the scripture in Luke 22:14." He added, "Institutions are a conveyance of substance, and after an institution is created; the substance starts to leak out. How can we do a better job of monitoring its purpose? One, the Oneness of Judaism. Two, the Unconditional Love of Christianity. Three, the Compassion of Islam." He added, "Jesus is for healing and freedom."

Imam Jamal said, "We're all seeking presence, to be conscious of God. When you are conscious of God, you are truly present and then the divine qualities can flow-they can flow only in the present moment." He added with humour,

"Blessed are the flexible for they will never get bent out of shape."

Together we sang, *Shalom (Hebrew), Salaam (Arabic), Peace.*

The Walk of Jesus with the Franciscan Monks

At 3 pm on Friday, I walked the Via Dolorosa, the Walk of Sorrows. In the October sun, a large crowd of us followed the Franciscan Monks in their brown robes through winding, uneven, bevelled-stone walkways of the Old City of Jerusalem. My one word in retrospect of this experience was "insane". I'm glad I went because the journey was through the market area. People were going in two different directions in the narrow streets that smelled of spices and body odours. Merchandise was often bright and glittery. The loud noise of aggressive selling was heard amid soft prayerful sounds.

At the beginning, we could hear the story of Jesus' walk in three languages; Hebrew, Arabic and English, with the monks quietly using their physical, prayerful presence to keep the procession in order. However, my attention was focused on safety for myself and my buddy so we wouldn't get lost. It became noisier with the people passing to and fro who were not participating in the walk. We couldn't hear the guiding words by the third station, out of fourteen Stations of the Cross. A motorcycle went by in the opposite direction a foot away from us. I became aware of how treacherous and frightening it must have been for Jesus. It also gave me a sense of how complicated life is in Jerusalem.

At the Church of the Holy Sepulchre where the walk ended, I lost my buddy amid the crushing crowd and décor of the Greek Orthodox Church. I went back to the open doorway of the church to wait for my buddy. An Episcopal priest from Ohio from our group waited with me. "How was the experience for you?" I shared I couldn't BE (meaning I couldn't be in an open contemplative mode as I had wished). He told me there was another opportunity to go early one morning with the person, who had been Dean of St George's College for thirty years. I called when back at the dorm to learn my buddy had gone ahead and was fine. I will include memories of the walk with the retired Dean a little later.

That evening, I journaled what I was yearning for to live more fully. I wrote. "I'm yearning for a spiritual, interfaith community that nurtures me in what God has given me, and gives me a place to use my gifts. I yearn for a community that is alive, where people know they are forgiven, have gratitude and express their joy. I want to express my joy! I want to continue to be consciously aware of God."

Bethlehem

On our way to Bethlehem by bus, we stopped at a field to plant an olive tree. It was energising and gratifying to dig a hole large enough in the dry, rocky soil for our young olive tree. We came with open, peace-filled, hopeful hearts, and the help of two Christian Palestinians. A nearby shepherd and sheep joined us. We dug, watered and planted the tree. The two Palestinians said they'd continue to care for the tree. The three amigos each said a prayer. We sang, *Shalom, Salaam, Peace.*

As we entered Bethlehem, I wondered what Jesus would think. There were stone and concrete buildings everywhere. There was evidence of violent destruction and litter.

The Church of the Nativity was under construction. As the legend says, the church is built over the cave where Jesus was born and laid in a manger. We wove in line through the scaffolding to an area surrounding the entry to the sacred space considered the scene of the nativity. To enter the Grotto of the Nativity, the crowd descended, one at a time, on semi-circular stone steps to a small entry – the Gate of Humility – about four feet tall. One person entered at a time, stooping to a bow through the doorway. There was a strong scent of incense. Once in, the ancient floor-space surrounded by inlaid paintings including a large silver star under the altar is considered to be where Jesus was born. Once I stooped to a bow through the Gate of Humility I got on my knees. I touched the Silver Star under the altar. I had to move quickly for the next person to enter. There's another passageway leading to an open area of stone caves. It gave a view of the kind of space where Joseph might have slept when he dreamed about Mary. It was real and surreal.

Palestine

We travelled to a two-story building that houses WI'AM, the Palestinian Conflict Resolution Centre. From the second story, we went further upstairs to an outside landing where the wind was cold. We saw many houses on hills, the beginning of a playground below, and an enormous grey metal wall with graffiti that said, among other things, "Bridges, not walls." An intimidating watchtower completed the metal wall.

We met a Palestinian peace worker. He said, "Any loss of a person is a loss to humanity. I am Isaac by the spirit (Christian), Ishmael (Arab) by the body. I believe in building bridges, not walls. The wall is a political wall." He said the resolution centre has a playground and is planting trees. He said they walk and talk non-violence and are destined to live together with diplomacy – Muslims, Jews and Christians. He said he chooses to help the weak and bring the strong to their senses. He said he can't go to Jerusalem without a permit and Israelis can't go to Bethlehem without a permit.

When asked what gives him hope, he said, "I am a student of history and know of the Berlin Wall, South African apartheid and Obama in the US. The door will open. Resurrection will come. The tomb will be empty. I can't live at the expense of others."

This eloquent man is an elected member of the city council, a minister and a religious counsellor. He said, "I want to live my life before my death." www.alaslah.org We gathered around him in the cold wind. Each interfaith amigo said a blessing, collectively putting their arms around him within our larger circle. All of us shed tears.

Somewhere on this day, Imam Jamal said, "Whose prisoner am I? Whose approval do I seek? Anyone whose approval you seek is your jailer; choose your jailers carefully." Imam Jamal added, "Spiritual poet Rumi, says compassion is the most important divine quality of life. Relate compassion to water in nature. There's nothing so soft and powerful. The most compassionate person is the most strong authentically, the most authentically life-affirming."

Whose prisoner am I, I asked myself? God's. I only want to be God's prisoner.

A Dream

The next morning, I awakened from a delightful dream. I was coming down an open wood staircase, about six steps from the bottom. There was soft light all around. I saw him coming toward the stair railing. It seemed it was intentional on his part. He was only inches away. We looked at each other and I gently said in surprised delight, "Dad." Dad smiled. He looked great with a younger, fuller face, his eyes soft, dark and sparkling. We embraced at that moment, physically and emotionally – an incredibly joyous moment. *Thank you, God.* I wept.

The Holocaust Museum

We travelled by bus to Yad Vashem, the Holocaust Museum. My new friend, a Jew, and I talked about our religions. We asked and answered each other's questions about faith. We laughed with love about our own inter-religious families.

The first part of the museum is in remembrance of the children who died in the Holocaust. I slowly walked into the dark area. A vast scene of space becomes filled with a multitude of stars hanging at eye level. Soft music played. I felt a choking sensation, amid open beauty.

The Walkway of the Righteous was an outside garden path with the names of people who helped the Jews. Names on plaques were interspersed between plants. It felt peaceful, honouring.

Inside the building were display panels with descriptions and photographs of the demeaning, cruel reality. When we entered this part of the museum, I decided I didn't need, nor want to feel the depth of pain today. I had already felt the anguish, anger, disgust, and wanton prayers for humanity at the Holocaust Museum in Washington, DC. I saw the museum with my youngest daughter when she graduated from high school – her request.

I went to Anne Frank's house in 1966 in Amsterdam, Holland, when my nurse friend and I went to Europe. One person guided us through the tiny house with its narrow staircase. I couldn't begin to imagine how a young girl, let alone how a family lived in quiet of voice and movement, in constant fear.

My husband and I had also been to the concentration camp in Dachau, Germany. I remember the many feet high surrounding grey cement walls; a creamy coloured gate that appeared deceptively welcoming. The railroad tracks – the deadly ride. Uninsulated wood buildings with three levels of narrow wooden bunk beds where two people laid in one bunk- with many sets in one room. A three-foot diameter circular washbasin for many. The solo prisoner cells. I thought of Lutheran Minister, and resister, Dietrich Bonhoeffer, his unwavering faith, in spite of humanity. The empty room with ceiling spigots for the unexpected shower of deadly gas – the agony. The open doors to the brick ovens with shovels waiting. Really? Really. It was abhorrent with shivers of disbelief, anger, and questions. How do we stop our fear of another, our dehumanising?

Shortly after I entered Yad Vashem Museum's main building, I noticed one of my fellow pilgrim's face of anguish. She was bent forward, hanging onto another pilgrim's arm. The other peer pilgrim was trying to look at the display. After seconds of wondering if I should or shouldn't, I decided to offer my arm to the struggling person. She took my arm. She shared she was dismayed with the visual pain of the Jews, and also thinking of the current oppression of the Palestinians. We'd been told to be silent throughout the museum. We'd been told there was a room where anyone could go if they needed a time apart. We went and sat in the peaceful area, however, my fellow pilgrim couldn't be silent. We went outside into the welcome sunshine. We sat on a curb and I listened. Being with her was where I was supposed to be.

That evening, Rabbi Ted said, "No one can kill unless they demonise the other. When the Jews were put in camps, their hair shorn, their clothes shabby and they were not able to bathe and change, they smelled and looked less. Then it's easier to kill. We've learned from history that we don't learn from history."

In addition, Rabbi Ted said, "The responsibility of the Jews of the Holocaust was denial. There was an unwillingness to believe. Jews were taken by surprise. We are asked not to deny, but to feel with one another." He said, "Jews would like the Holocaust to be called, the Shoa, because it means destruction; not sacrifice, which is what holocaust means."

The Second Walk of the Via Delarosa

At 5:45 Monday morning, we interested pilgrims gathered outside the cathedral. We met our learned, faith-filled guide. Our guide was retiring from his position of thirty years as Dean of St George's College in Jerusalem. The journey of the Walk of Sorrows with him was a generous gift. He explained that we don't know the true steps of Jesus. They would be several feet below us. However, he said his hope was each of us would leave a grain of sand from our shoes on the path.

In quiet, seven of us followed and listened. We listened with all our senses as we wound through the Old City and the fourteen stations. He said, "Nine of the stations come from the gospels. Five come from medieval European imagination: Jesus' three falls, his meeting his mother, and Veronica wiping Jesus' face." He brought a wooden cross. We took turns carrying the cross. He explained Jesus would have carried a cross beam that would be nailed to a tree, not a full cross, but still heavy.

The markets were opening. Whenever anyone greeted our guide, he returned a greeting in their language, blessed with a tone of high regard. He pointed out a man sweeping up bread crumbs and putting them to the side in his marketplace. He told us a Muslim doesn't throw away any bread or rice because it is food for life. As our pilgrim from Ireland carried the cross, I was moved by the telling of his wounds. I became aware of my own wounds.

At the tiny house entry of Veronica (now a food pantry), our guide stood on the simple house stoop facing us. He talked softly. He took his hand and gently touched me under my chin. He did the same to another pilgrim. While looking into my eyes, he softly and convincingly said, "You are the face of God."

We ended our walk at an empty tomb in the Church of the Holy Sepulchre. Because of the crowds and losing my buddy I didn't know about or see the tomb on my first walk. As our learned guide said, "What other church, what other cathedral, what other basilica in the world hosts an empty tomb? None other does. Such a church is found only in Jerusalem. Our roots stem from this empty tomb."

I got to crouch and enter the tomb. The entry had a flat area for a person to bring spices and have a little room to move around. I didn't know that after a period of years, a tomb was cleared of the remnants and used again.

At our guide's quiet request we hummed, *Christ the Lord Is Risen Today* (Wesley, Charles). Suddenly we heard grand, joyous organ music awakening tears of my awe and joy. He told us how candles were lit on Easter morning and sent around the world.

We had twenty minutes after our walk to hustle back to the college, have a quick breakfast and grab our belongings to get on the bus to go to the Dead Sea. Prior to the pilgrimage, I decided to bring my paintbrush, watercolours and a plastic cup to paint with the saltwater from the Dead Sea.

The Dead Sea – Qumran – My Scroll

The Dead Sea is at least 300 feet below sea level. It is surrounded by white desert sand. The mud of the Dead Sea is black and is said to have healing qualities. Many people put on their swimsuits, floated in the water and covered themselves with black mud. It was hot. I sat under an umbrella and painted. The water felt sticky. There was no green foliage surrounding the lake, however, the sky was blue. The sun sparkled on the water. Black mud was evident on my fellow pilgrims frolicking or floating in the sea. I felt joy and peace as I brushed a simple dream come true with black figures in the sea.

As we left the Dead Sea, I noted the highway signs. One said Jerusalem, the other said, Jericho. *I feel like I'm living in a storybook...oh yeah, the Bible.*

We travelled a short distance in the vast limestone desert with magnificent pink and yellow ochre-coloured hills with darker valleys. Goats were grazing though it didn't look like there was anything for them to eat. We stopped at Qumran where the Dead Sea Scrolls were found in 1947, because of a goat's wandering and a shepherd who entered a cave.

While at Qumran we were asked to write our own scroll, imagining we had written it many years ago. My scroll said you are my daughter (God's daughter). You belong to me. Anything you do will be adequate. The word adequate caught me; then I thought, *yes, adequate is good. I don't have to be perfect.*

The Dome of the Rock –
The Western Wall

Back in Jerusalem, we wore headscarves out of respect for other women, to visit the Dome of the Rock at Temple Mount. Again, the Dome of the Rock is an Islamic sacred site. It wasn't open to the public because of recent violence. It stood majestically in detailed coloured mosaic tiles in an open space inviting quiet roaming. I experienced inner peace as I walked and stood in shadows.

From the Dome of the Rock, we walked the short distance to the Western Wall after going through security. From the suspended walkway, we could see the tall stone wall with men and women praying in separate places. Rabbi Ted encouraged us to look for a place where we could actually press our bodies against the wall to pray and to put our written prayer in a crevice. I looked for a crevice for my prayer, and for my friend from Minnesota who mailed her prayer to me. I had carried my friend's prayer next to me until this moment. I knew Helen held me in prayer, too. I held her preciously written and delicately packaged prayer in my hand. I chose a beckoning spot. I guess it chose me. I prayerfully, securely tucked the prayer into the dark open crevice. What was most moving for me was I could fulfil Helen's request, as someone had filled my request years before.

At the end of the day, I thought, *it's not about sacred sites. What's most meaningful is each person's journey, brought by the invitation to faith, and the deepening of faith. To me, we, all people everywhere, journey with the Transcendent and to the Transcendent in our own way.*

Nazareth

We leave Jerusalem and head into the Judean desert. We saw the Jordan River on our right. A military jeep with four soldiers in it was driving next to the barbed wire fence on our side of the river. A rake on the side of the jeep aligned the sand so the soldiers could easily see if anyone cleared the fence. How *sad,* remembering Dalia Landau's words.

While travelling we asked how the three amigos deal with people who disagree with them. They said they listen and do not express any judgement. Get to know someone on a personal level, they said. Jamal added, "Share three cups of tea while listening." They referred to Gandhi who said, '*To create peace, it's the sacred duty of a person to be aware of the other person's religion.*' Acknowledge every single religion has truths and non-truths.

The amigos said what they have found most surprising is how their experiences have enriched their own paths. The open-table, intense acceptance, appreciation and – the outrageous opens us to something new they said. When we're friends, we can name the difficulties and different perceptions.

We travelled three hours north to Nazareth. We travelled through the flat land, hill, then desert to the fertile valley and green. We saw the Sea of Galilee. Our bus driver stopped. We waded in the clear water of the Sea of Galilee. A Presbyterian minister asked me to baptise her. As the warm sun glistened on the still waters, my hand brought drips of the water of Galilee to her forehead. I said the gratefully remembered words. I asked her to do the same for me. A therapist from Vancouver asked me to baptise her. I did and she said, "Your energy is beautiful. Thank you." I noticed Imam Jamal knee-deep in the water with his pant legs rolled up and thought how dear, how lovely. Here we all are: Muslim, Jew and Christian in the Sea of Galilee wading in joyous peace.

We stopped at a Benedictine Monastery. It is a modern building with windows facing the waters of Galilee. The monastery is a retreat centre, too. We had lunch, with coffee on the stone deck facing the sea. I had pictures taken with arms around new friends from Boston, Massachusetts, Ireland, and South Africa.

We stopped at Safed, the city of Jewish mystics. The Jewish Mystics date back to the 16th C. Rabbi Isaac Luria (Ari) who lived 400 years ago is buried there. He died in 1572 at the age of 38.

We arrived in Nazareth in darkness. We stayed our last two nights at the Convent of the sisters of Nazareth who came to Nazareth around 1883. They were originally founded in France. The convent was an old school, now used for hospitality.

My room was on the third floor where a double door opened to an area that is the roof of the convent. I stepped into the darkness and saw the brightness of the stars with a crescent moon over homes and churches on the hillside. I reaped the amazement of having looked at the stars in Jerusalem, at home in North Carolina, and now in Nazareth.

The Beatitudes – Our Goodbyes

Our pilgrimage would soon end. We drove to the Mount of the Beatitudes. Road signs throughout our entire trip have been in Hebrew, Arabic and English. The area of the Mount of Beatitudes is gorgeous with its lush grounds of trees, flowers and birds. The beatitudes were written on stones placed throughout the grounds. We had time to walk from stone to stone.

In a small area with a stone table and stone benches, all of us sat under trees that cast shadows through the streams of sunlight. We sat to hear our treasured amigo friends once more, knowing we would soon part.

We heard that prophets don't have congregations. I paused and thought of Jesus, our amigos, and my own life. We were reminded the core teachings were about: The oneness of the Jewish tradition; the Unconditional Love of Christianity; Compassion in Islam.

"Be wary when you think you know the answer. The beatitudes don't rely on rationality; we need heart and soul," said Pastor Don.

Jamal reminded us that surrender to God is crucial, "Help me God," he said. Again, he reminded us, "Remember whosever approval you seek; they are your jailor; choose well."

Yes, I say to myself, as I think, remembering scripture (Luke 18:29-30) from Jesus about leaving your parents, brother, sister, all. It's that same meaning to me. I need only God's approval. It can be lonely, but I'm never alone. (America)

We returned to the convent in Nazareth and shared our final meditation and blessings. We pilgrims led a thank you and blessing for the three amigos. One pilgrim spoke of her fond, life-giving relationships with the three amigos. Another pilgrim read words from a basket filled with one meaningful word we each put in the basket; my word was Via Delarosa. As the third person to facilitate our goodbye, I then explained the olive tree concepts Jamal had shared: the roots of the tree grow deep, it takes a long time to grow, the branches and leaves may struggle, and even have pain as they appear and are pruned. I bowed facing the amigos, accompanied by all pilgrims, as I ended with Jamal's words, "When the tree bears fruit, it bows in gratitude and humility." We ended in song, in Hebrew, Arabic and English.

In the morning, Christian Church bells rang simultaneously as the Muslim prayer was spoken. I looked at the morning sun on the houses and churches on the hills of Nazareth, in awe. *I'm in Nazareth; soon to leave this living dream.*

○

Back in the United States and we enter another subject. Grandchildren arrived in my sixties after I'd moved to North Carolina with my new husband. The grandchildren were in another state however, it was an enticing doable six-hour drive from our North Carolina home. It was a labour of love to visit every two weeks. I loved it. I loved seeing and holding our new babies, twin girls, feeling their sweet breath on my neck as I held their warm bodies. Sometimes I held both of them at once.

I accompanied my daughter when she took the twin girls to the doctor after they'd been home a short while to make sure they were doing all right. When discharged from the hospital after a month, the girls were to be kept in a darkened room, together in one crib. This was to resemble the still needed time of growth in the womb, as they were premature. When the physician lifted one of the twins and held her in front of her, the baby brought up her arm to cover her face. The doctor said, "See, she can stand to look only at her mother's face, but no other yet." I thought, isn't that like us with God. We can't handle seeing all of God at once.

Less than two years later, they had another girl. Now we had a joyful, consuming trio.

When our twin girls were six years old and their sister four years old, I stayed with them on Easter weekend. My three granddaughters and I had spent enough time together with and without Mum and Dad, that the girls were comfortable with just us. Knowing I would be there for a weekend, I brought props for playtime. To have fun.

My mum had worn hats. I saved a few of my mum's belongings after her death at age ninety-five. Mum did change in her last few years. She became a caring listener. She laughed with appreciation when she had two Great Granddaughters. She shone with delight when I showed her a Christmas purchase of red velvet outfits. The outfits were to be from her for the babies' first Christmas.

One of Mum's hats was formed red-felt with an upturned brim made to fit securely. The other, also red, was soft and floppy. In addition, I had a multi-layered hat that looked like pink, yellow and peach flower petals. It was given to me by a North Carolina friend who knew I loved hats. My friend had quoted the opinion that "under every cute hat was a great woman." Amen, I say. I had Mum's well-cared-for cotton dress gloves in white, summer green and red.

My mechanical engineer husband had rescued a discarded pink, battery-powered buggy from a happy donor. He put a new battery in the buggy. He washed and rubbed it dry. We had previously brought it to the girls in Maryland in my husband's truck. The girls weren't sure what to do with the buggy. It was kept under the back porch and used with assistance over the tiny hills and valleys of the large, lush lawn. Their parents didn't have time or energy to spend in buggy time.

The family of three girls also had a new addition, Yappy. We weren't sure what her final name would be, but Yappy was it for now. Yappy, a Yorkie, about five years old, was rescued by the vet my daughter and husband used for years for their dogs and cats. After the vet had Yappy for two weeks with no inquiries, even from the rescue organisations, the vet asked if the family would foster her. And so, it was. Yappy and the girls loved each other.

Easter morning the girls were surprised when they discovered Easter baskets filled with a large chocolate bunny, candy Easter eggs and miniature toy people and animals. Expressions of the joy of the sights and the taste of chocolate before breakfast were abundant. All the girls said Mum and Dad would be surprised when they got home to learn of finding Easter treats.

Later that morning, I brought out the bag of props. Eager faces, with noses in the bag, watched as the zipper opened. As each item appeared, it immediately went on a head or hand as they giggled and looked at me and each other for the nod of, "Yes, it's perfect for you." Each girl now had a new outfit for the day accompanied by hats and gloves.

I told them my story of the Easter Parade as I remembered the song and the newspaper photos. I sang the song, *In your Easter bonnet with all the frills upon it, you'll be the grandest lady in the Easter parade.* I told them everyone got dressed up for Easter when I was a young girl. The ladies wore hats and gloves. Girls had new dresses and shoes. Men wore suits and ties. Boys wore bright shirts and new trousers. Many people went to church in their finery. It's been said in stories that a photographer with a large black camera walked around the parade snapping pictures as people walked to church.

Everyone in the parade smiled, loving the sunshine, the scents, and the budding flowers. Everyone was happy to be together, realising spring was blossoming.

I told the girls the hats and gloves, now theirs, had belonged to my mum, their great-grandmother; a new concept to them. Their twinkling eyes gave an appreciative, gleeful look.

Desire brought grins of impatience. We ran into the inviting, sunny day. On to the freedom of green grass and a slightly bumpy yard. Yappy joined us. The girls' energy propelled their lean bodies, powered by partially eaten chocolate bunnies. I managed to get the pink open buggy moved from under the porch. Jovial sounds prevailed as they each hopped in. Two in the front and one standing in the back. I sang the Easter Parade song with gusto. The three young girls dressed as gorgeous, confident ladies were now genuinely in the parade. As the buggy slowly moved, they waved to everyone showing off their finery, and enjoying the imaginary fans. They showed off their modelling selves for the attentive running photographer trying to keep up with the buggy. I, their adoring grandmother, was their most enthusiastic fan as I waved, laughed and smiled in ecstasy. I described the pretend scene envisioned for the next day's newspaper with their photos.

I announced, "Three wild ladies with life glistening in their eyes spread a glow wherever they went. They were dressed in red, pink and green with hats and gloves to match. A crazy dog called Yappy with high pointed ears ran ahead of them, then back, ahead again, excitedly barking, announcing the joyful trio. The fashion police wanted to catch up to them. People stopped, looked and waved; they were compelled by the treasured enthusiasm. Nothing else mattered, the crowd wanted to drop all duties, their work, run after the ladies and join in the liveliness. Mothers ran with their babies in strollers. Babies belly-laughed with glee. Horses whinnied and cows mooed."

On the slippery grass shining with pearls of dew, the ladies stopped under tall trees that supported two cardinals, mourning doves and a robin singing, all in tune. Standing first, then one foot at a time, they each got out of the buggy. One was in black high heels that clicked when she walked. The other with red boots that sang. The other with black, high boots with shiny diamonds that reflected the sunlight. The ladies gently handled buds on the apple, pear and cottonwood trees. An enchanted swing hung on a long thick rope from the tallest branch allowing each one to swing far and wide. Yappy sat panting. Suddenly, all three ran to the buggy, beckoned by its dimming headlights. The last I saw; the three young ladies were still waving.

O

My ageing face looks back at me in the magnifying mirror. I put on make-up "to look alive", my mum would say. Make-up involves a soft line of lipstick lightened by my index finger wiping colour from my lips to dab on my pale cheeks. Next, I apply a little eyebrow pencil to give me eyebrows where they have almost disappeared. Then it looks like I have eyes, even when I can't see well anymore due to macular degeneration.

I see enough to know the mirror is cruel. At age 76, the contours of my face reveal ageing lines across my forehead. Curved lines outline my eyes. The curves go up to show interest and a smile – not a frown and anxiety. My chin is plumped below the lower lip showing it off, making up for my thin upper lip. A grey cap I wear for gardening says, "I don't remember asking for wrinkles when I grew up."

I recall a woman in her nineties, who was a resident in a skilled long-term care facility. She briskly lifted and set her walker down in a mission-driven fashion. She walked her small frame into my brightly lit office. She exclaimed in anxiety-filled words she didn't have money to pay for lunch. I invited her to sit on the green upholstered chair facing my desk. She did.

I got on my knees on the carpet facing her. While she rested her arms on her silver-coloured walker, her troubled eyes peered at me through the spaces. I asked her what was happening. She repeated her concern. I told her lunch was already paid for, aware confusion and memory issues were part of her disease. I didn't know if she'd believe me. I noticed her short white wispy hair surrounding her oval-shaped face. Her face was a pattern of lifelines that gave her glowing beauty. As I looked into her eyes, I thought, *when I'm ninety, I hope I look like you.* Our eyes met, deeply met. Our souls touched one another; Eucharist.

My granddaughter says I look like a bird. I have a wattle under my chin she loves to stroke. As she lays her head in my lap, and gently swabs her seven-year-old finger across the flesh, she says, "You have wrinkles, Gramma. It is soft." My upper arms have fleshy wings that I work out to keep in flight. My granddaughters and I dance and sing to John Denver's capturing music.

Now I'm the elderly. It's fun and it's hard. I wouldn't trade these years after 60. I have reasonable health and money to live on so far. I learned from the elderly that faith, fun and flexibility are keys to healthy living. Since my fall and rise from the spiritual bottom, I have fulfilling interests where there is no monetary payment.

I've let go of what I've outgrown. Sometimes that's even a friend. I keep doing what I love such as writing; painting watercolours and acrylics, and over and over seeking a new dream to see my family again.

As I said earlier, I gave up dreams when I hit the bottom of the well. However, well water runs deep and keeps abundance in mind for us when we think all is lost.

As a friend said, "Lake Superior is your inner landscape." Every time I'm near Lake Superior, near the green spruce and white birch trees, I eagerly wait for the second I can get out of the car. I run to the lake. Yes, I still run. My yearning hands scoop up the cool water. I re-baptise myself with Lake Superior's life-giving water.

○

"Mum, you've got to fight," my son said.

In earnest, I replied, "I want to live another twenty years. There's a lot I want to do yet. You may even want to shoot me if I live so long," I said with a laugh. "However, this is my reality, my choice."

The novel Coronavirus, COVID-19, has affected my husband of 18 years, and me since the end of February 2020. We were to take our last (last, because of the length of plane trips and our ages of 76 and 77), dream trip in March going to Australia and New Zealand. Going around New Zealand and coming back home were to be by cruise ship.

After listening to my three adult children's concerns and the daily news indicating the virus was dangerous for the elderly and those with pre-existing conditions, we cancelled our trip. If we hadn't, we might still be on that cruise ship.

Hundreds of thousands of people in the United States have been deathly ill, dying, of COVID-19. Globally, millions more are sick. It is a nasty virus, described as pernicious and quick. A person can be asymptomatic, unknowingly spreading the virus. We're learning the virus not only affects the lungs, causing a respiratory illness, but it affects the heart and ultimately all vital organs.

People who are extremely ill with a fever and difficulty breathing because of COVID-19 are admitted to the hospital, alone. No one can accompany them. Otherwise, the accompanying person can bring more COVID into the hospital, or catch the virus there, and spread the virus to their family and other unsuspecting people. A ventilator is often needed to assist breathing to the keep lungs and other vital organs alive. Ventilators for patients and protective equipment such as masks and gowns for doctors, nurses and cleaning staff were initially in short supply. This is an unconscionable situation of lack of preparedness for any pandemic on the part of our federal government in 2020.

No family member can accompany the dying patient either. It is the desire of any nurse to be with a dying patient if the family can't be there. Because of the number of critically ill patients, nurses have the frustration of not being able to provide the care they know is best. This is emotionally wounding for everyone. The family of the deceased cannot be together for a funeral except virtually by technology. This is a nightmare for anyone, patients, staff, families and our economy. Any healing of these wounds will take decades when we begin to heal. A year since the virus started, healing is not in sight, though vaccination has started.

As a person and as a nurse, I pondered and envisioned the above-described situations from both angles. After days of serious consideration, I told my adult children that if I got the virus, I did not want to go to the hospital. I want to stay quarantined at home, where there's a bedroom window, to be able to see my family. I knew I might change my mind depending on how hard it was to breathe. "If I do enter a hospital," I said, "I don't want to be put on a ventilator." Being ventilated doesn't guarantee full recovery. At this stage in life, I said, "let me go, let me die."

That's when my son said, "Mum, you've got to fight."

I realised in my quandary, there are probably many who have wondered the same thing. We don't talk about death and our wishes in this country. Lots of people don't want to consider they're going to die someday. Deciding how you would choose to die, (given the choice), is usually not the desired discussion.

There ARE choices. My family is aware of my Advanced Directives indicating my wishes if terminally ill or not being able to speak on my own. I have appointed who (and an alternate) will have power of attorney. My son and I haven't talked at length about death. I think we need to discuss it more. Imagining our own death, that reality is part of being willing to discuss options with personal views and choices on how we want to die.

Our first responders: People, who drive buses, work in grocery stores, meat processing plant workers, as well as our EMTs, physicians, and nurses, are all at great risk. The numbers who have died keeps increasing.

We are restricted certainly, but my husband and I have our own interests and spaces within our home. We are retired. Because I'm accustomed to time alone, and now enjoy it; I don't feel stripped of activities as many do. I can't imagine being in love and not being able to be together. I can't imagine not being able to visit a loved one in a nursing home or in the hospital. I can't imagine having to go to work, especially in a risky situation of a hospital or meatpacking plant, and have children who need care at home. I can't imagine being unemployed, standing in line for hours, and having no other support.

It is painful to not be able to see our families and friends, to hug them, to support and celebrate with them. My arms ache for those loves.

Electronically, we've been able to meet by Zoom, which enables us to see and talk with each other virtually. Our grandchildren are changing and growing by the second; we don't want to miss a once in a lifetime milestone.

The goodness evident is people are more kind to one another with a wave or hello when I take my morning solo walk always staying the distance. Our five-year-old and two-year-old grandsons wave, blow kisses, and send very big hugs trying to knock me over from many feet away. They laugh as I pretend to fall as I receive their hugs and kisses from a great distance. My granddaughters; twins 12 and younger 11 have zoomed with us. They include their dog, (now called Sunny), their guinea pigs Maple and Dandy and their newest family member, guinea pig, Trixie. Our eight-year-old grandson and two-year-old granddaughter, with a computer in hand last summer, showed us the bright sun gleaming on the blue water. Now, in mid-winter, they share their drawings of a snowman. There are lots of "I love you" in our texts.

The air is cleaner, even evident in just months after COVID started, in photos over Los Angeles, Paris, Venice and even Wuhan, China, where it is thought the virus started.

During this time, I think of the words, '*All will be well*' by Julian of Norwich (England) who lived in the 14th C. The bubonic plague and other strife were in England and in Europe at the time.

I know God is a mystery and there will be more goodness that comes out of this COVID 19 reflective time.

We continue in the between space of what's been, what will never be again; what is, and wondering what will be. It is a time of quiet and reflection for some. For some, it's a time of frantic living, of grieving death. It's a time that's demonstrated the disparities in our nation. More people of colour, especially black people are dying of COVID-19. Many people of colour are first responders and health care providers. Decades of lack of healthcare coverage, education and job opportunities are still prevalent.

In the early months of our isolation in 2020, our son-in-law texted me to say if I would like to call and explain about the candle I left at their door, I could call now. How excited I was to talk with my grandson who I missed terribly. My five-year-old grandson said, "Mummy sometimes works on Friday but she doesn't have to work Friday (it's now Wednesday). We're going to have a picnic. (The picnic will be inside, on a blanket on the floor – a remembered event for me) Today we're going to make the house sparkle."

"Sparkle," I responded. "I love that word."

"We clean from the ceiling to the floor," he continued. "We don't want to clean low first because gravity makes things fall down and we'd have more again. I love you, Grandma." I melted with smiles from our sparkling conversation.

Younger two-year-old brother chimed in, "Fall down. Grandma, love you." *Ooooh*, I thought, as my heart yearned.

I envisioned their dad's phone was on their oval-shaped dining table. Each son was in a chair at opposite ends of the table. Our oldest grandson said, "He's in a booster seat with a strap. I am too. I don't have a strap."

"The candle I left at your door in a paper bag is yours to keep," I said. "You know how to turn it off and on. You can do that anytime. If you're wondering about Grandma and Grandpa, just turn it on and know we're thinking of you," I said this, knowing candlelit and silent thoughts projected help me. For my emotional health, and I hope for his, I left a battery-powered candle at the door because the day before I was sad thinking this little guy loves to be with people. He needed his friends and he couldn't right now. School has changed dramatically. I miss hearing from my granddaughters too. They have renewed smartphones with FaceTime ability so I was investigating phone possibilities for me. I think we'd talk more if we could see each other.

My grandson continued, "Mum and I bake. We had blueberry short—"

"—cake," his dad says from the background.

"Yeah, it was a blueberry shortcake with REAL whipped cream." I added, "It looked so good. I wanted to reach over and get a blueberry." (Our families had a zoom birthday celebration for my 49-year-old son in Minnesota. Each family had a dessert to eat in their own home while on zoom) "Remember when you made your brother's cake for his first birthday?" I said laughing a bit, visualising it again.

"Yeah, he had his hands all squishy with the cake and frosting," he said with light laughter.

Younger brother added, "Cake...I wanna talk, Grandma," he longingly said with an anguished, frustrated tone. My heart wanted to run the two blocks to their home and embrace him. I greeted him while trying to think of what I could do next to connect while invisible.

"Do you sing with your dad? Can you both sing something like Twinkle, twinkle little star?" I asked.

"No, but we know another song about Ella." I think he said Ella. I listened to his full voice singing stanzas. On occasion, I could hear another sound from his younger brother, how dear. We didn't know a sweet note was incubating; a baby, expected in the spring.

With emptiness in my heart, I say to myself; we grandmothers and grandchildren mutually contribute to the life and welfare of all. Grandmothers know life is fragile and precious, yet strong with never-ending effects. We are being ripped off. So many in so many ways are being ripped off.

COVID-19 is a never-ending fog. It's filled with bone-chilling sadness. Its heaviness snuffs the life out of nurses who are in it up to their grief-filled eyeballs. Nurses and Certified Nursing Assistants labour with patients and residents for minutes, days, weeks, months, and years now. Some doctors have left their families and stayed in a nearby hotel to the hospital because they worked such long hours, and didn't want to expose their families to the virus. These realities of life are intimate. The moments of laughter, the moments of tears, the soul-to-soul moments aren't forgotten.

In these difficult times, it's not unusual to ask where God is. Does God exist? Scripture tells us we have free will. God doesn't promise a smooth ride in life. We make choices. Some choices end up being death-producing; like some I've made. What God did/does promise is God is always with us; not to fear. I still fear at times. I'm human. If I remember and allow God to be with me, fear is alleviated. Strength and courage come. Healthier choices are made.

Covid 2021

The virus has mutated more than once, enlivening variants.

We still have people in powerful congressional offices who DON'T CARE ENOUGH to say the TRUTH about the seriousness of the virus, and the need to vaccinate.; to say to those they represent. "WE have an infectious disease we must fight. We fight it by wearing a mask (or two). Stay apart from others when away from home. If it's necessary to be with someone, again, wear a mask. I, CARE ENOUGH about YOU, to change our course, to wear a mask myself, and ask you to wear one, too."

Each of us who gets vaccinated helps stop the virus from spreading, to break the chain of infection. It IS the most LOVING thing we can do.

Now, in 2022, over a million people have died in the United States alone. Our family is experiencing the loss of a loved one too. One of our grandchildren died. I can't begin to tell the story of that precious life and death at this time. I hope, the mother of this child, my daughter, will write that story.

The fog only intermittently lifts, letting the sun of gratitude in.

○

For nearly fifty years, I hoped my family would attend church together.

It happened, at United Church of Christ with our pastor's blessing, via zoom, on July 26, 2020. In our morning service, the Co-founder of the International Crane Foundation (ICF) was our virtual guest telling the story in voice, and visually, of the come-back of the almost extinct Whooping Cranes. Going from about 15 Whooping Cranes in 1940 to Whooping Cranes now living in the wild in Wisconsin, raising their own chicks. It's taken years of science, the dedication of many, and global support for all of life.

In 2016, I saw the last minutes of a Public Broadcasting Service (PBS) presentation. It showed the spring migration of the Sandhill Cranes flying into the Platte River in Nebraska. The sky was pink, yellow, blue and grey. In the broadcast, I witnessed thousands of birds with their wings extended; their wings lowering; and finally, their magnificent bodies settling into the reflecting river water. I gasped in awe, overflowing with wanton joy. I wanted the sight to last forever. Their flight into the river took flight in me. Their beings captured my heart.

I went on to learn more at the International Crane Foundation in Baraboo, Wisconsin, Co-founded by Ron

Sauey (deceased), and Dr George Archibald. It's 50 minutes from our Wisconsin home. Anticipating seeing the 15 species of cranes, I took my dragonfly-embossed covered backpack, just the perfect size for postcard-sized watercolours. My mini watercolour set (a gift from my husband); a bottle of water and one brush was enough to start a painting. Excitement entered as I drove into the parking lot. The Cerulean Blue sky was partly cloudy.

I walked the grounds seeing all the cranes. At the Whooping Crane exhibit, I sat on a wooden seat in the open sheltered area watching two glorious-white five-foot-tall cranes. Both were gently, yet purposefully moving their long thin black legs, seeking food by lowering their red-topped heads and long bills into the water. It was peaceful and radiant with beauty; I didn't want to leave. I didn't paint. I sat there in the beloved silence of the majesty of God.

In the gift shop, I purchased the book, *My Life with Cranes*, by George Archibald. It is one of the most inspiring books I've ever read. Co-founder and author, George Archibald, clearly listened to his heart throughout his life. His passion, commitment, and energy, with faith, led him to choices that has brought gifts to all of us, globally.

I wanted our church youth to be aware of the concept of extinction by creating a picture of an animal they would miss. A parishioner took on this challenge with creativity and zeal.

All my grandchildren, their art, and their parents were present, along with forty other people. The visuals of the Whooping Cranes along with the engagement and storytelling and children's art were inspiring; a dream come true and better than I ever imagined.

○

For a girl who couldn't speak, I've had a lot to say. Who would ever believe I would write; and write about God?

Holy longings are formed in the womb.

The deepest, most authentic longing was heeded by the young girl, searching. Though her image of a loving God became tainted with oppression, fear, perfectionism and self-rejection, entombing her, seeking prevailed.

The longing is forever pure, though hidden. In our darkness of the tomb, transformation happens. We are resurrected. We have a new beginning. It's as though, we again, or maybe always, are in the womb of God.

God takes our woundedness, and with a silent tear or rushing waterfall, turns it into our gift, our strength.

Works Cited

The New Oxford Annotated Bible with the Apocrypha, REVISED STANDARD VERSION BIBLE, NY 1977 by Oxford University Press Inc. by Division of Christian Education of the National Council of Churches of Christ in the United States of America.

Irving Berlin, the song, EASTER PARADE, was written by Irving Berlin, published in 1933. (Used on page 196 of the story.)

Cameron, Julia, THE ARTIST'S WAY A SPIRITUAL PATH TO HIGHER CREATIVITY, NY, Putnam's Sons, 1992 p 9

Carol Hymowitz and Michaele Weissman, A History of Women in America, Bantam Books Inc., 666 Fifth Avenue, New York, NY, 1978 by the Anti-Defamation League of B'nai B'rith (pages 123-126)

Cogger, Dawn, "God Meets Us Where We Are: The Spiritual Director Continues to Heal," the article was FIRST PUBLISHED in PRESENCE, AN INTERNATIONAL

JOURNAL OF SPIRITUAL DIRECTION, Vol. 6, NO 2, June 2010, in Bellevue, WA, pp 46, 103

English, John, S.J., SPIRITUAL FREEDOM, FROM AN EXPERIENCE OF THE IGNATIOAN EXERCISES TO THE ART OF SPIRITUAL DIRECTION, Loyola House, Guelph, Ontario, Canada, 1987, pp 14-21

Fish, Sharon, and Shelly, Judith Allen, SPIRITUAL CARE THE NURSES ROLE, Intervarsity Press, Downers Grove, Illinois, 1978, pp. 46, 47

Guenther, Margaret, HOLY LISTENING THE ART OF SPIRITUAL DIRECTION, Cowley Publications, Boston, Massachusetts, 1992, p 3

Linn, Dennis; Sheila Fabricant Linn; and Matthew Linn. SLEEPING WITH BREAD: HOLDING WHAT GIVES YOU LIFE. New York, NY: Paulist Press, 1995, pp 6,7

Miller, Alice, THE DRAMA OF THE GIFTED CHILD, New York, NY: Basic Books, 2008. First published in English as PRISONERS OF CHILDHOOD, by Basic Books, Inc., of New York in 1981. Originally published in German as DAS DRAMA DES BEGABTEN KIDES in 1979, Suhrkamp Verlag Frankfurt am Main.

Nell Irvin Painter, SOJOURNER TRUTH, A LIFE, A SYMBOL, W. W. Norton & Company, Inc., 500 Fifth Avenue, New York, NY, 10110. 1996

Notes

[1] Elizabeth O'Conner, OUR MANY SELVES, New York, NY, Harper & Row, 1971.

[2] The Cenacle Spiritual Direction Training Program, Sisters of the Cenacle that were in Wayzata, Minnesota can now be reached at cenaclesisters.org in Chicago, Illinois.

[3] Church Publishing Incorporated, HOLY WOMEN, HOLY MEN, CELEBRATING THE SAINTS, Church Publishing Incorporated, New York, 2010.

[4] Pastor Don Mackenzie, Rabbi Ted Falcon and Imam Jamal Rahman, FINDING PEACE THROUGH SPIRITUAL PRACTICE, SKYLIGHTS PATHS, Nashville, Tennessee, 2016.

Notes

Ingram Content Group UK Ltd.
Milton Keynes UK
UKHW020923160323
418667UK00015B/1251